Are We Bodies or Souls?

Are We Bodies or Souls?

Richard Swinburne

OXFORD
UNIVERSITY PRESS

OXFORD
UNIVERSITY PRESS

Great Clarendon Street, Oxford, OX2 6DP,
United Kingdom

Oxford University Press is a department of the University of Oxford.
It furthers the University's objective of excellence in research, scholarship,
and education by publishing worldwide. Oxford is a registered trade mark of
Oxford University Press in the UK and in certain other countries

First Edition published in 2019
Impression: 1

Published in the United States of America by Oxford University Press
198 Madison Avenue, New York, NY 10016, United States of America

British Library Cataloguing in Publication Data
Data available

Library of Congress Control Number: 2019934392

ISBN 978-0-19-883149-5

Printed and bound in Great Britain by
Clays Ltd, Elcograf S.p.A.

Contents

1

Introduction

A. What This Book Is About

This book is about the nature of human beings, persons of the biological species to which we belong.[1] I have aimed to make my treatment of this topic accessible to readers from any background, but also one containing new philosophical material, whose central arguments academic philosophers and scientists will—I hope—find challenging.

On one view called 'physicalism' or 'materialism', we humans are physical substances (= physical objects or things), machines differing from other machines only by being much more complicated and made of flesh and blood rather than plastic and silicon chips. In this book I shall argue that as conscious rational agents, we are beings of a very different kind from inanimate physical substances. Our bodies may be for the most part very complicated machines; yet we ourselves are not such machines, but essentially non-physical beings: souls who control bodies. This view is a version of what is called 'substance dualism'; it holds that each of us living on earth consists of two distinct substances (two distinct parts)—body and soul, but the part that makes us who we are is our soul. Bodies keep us alive, and by enabling us to interact with each other and the world make our lives so greatly worth living; but souls are what we essentially are. By some miracle we might continue to exist without our body, but no miracle would make it possible for us to exist without our soul—because for each of us our soul is the one essential part of us.

Physicalism and substance dualism are both very old views. The 'atomists' of fifth-century BCE Greece, such as Democritus, advocated physicalism, while their far more famous near-contemporary Plato advocated substance dualism. Yet the great modern reverence for the recent achievements of the physical and biological sciences has led to the view that those sciences can explain everything, and so we must be things of the kind that they can explain—physical substances. Hence the current dominance of physicalism (= materialism) in the intellectual world. The American philosopher John Searle has written that 'There is a sense in which materialism is the religion of our time, at least among most of the professional experts in the fields of philosophy, psychology, cognitive science, and other disciplines that study the mind. Like more traditional religions, it is accepted without question and it provides the framework within which other questions can be posed, addressed, and answered'.[2]

I shall be arguing that none of the enormous achievements of modern physical and biological sciences, which we all so rightly revere, provide or could provide in future any reason at all for denying the crucial difference between humans and inanimate physical objects analysed by the version of substance dualism which I shall advocate; and that substance dualism is the only theory of human nature which takes serious account of all the data of neuroscience and human experience. Although I shall also be discussing other views of human nature, intermediate between physicalism and my version of substance dualism, it is because the most prominent rival view to mine is the physicalism that claims that we are essentially bodies, and the view which I shall advocate that we are essentially souls, that I have given the book the title 'Are We Bodies or Souls?' Substance dualism is a view available both to religious believers and to atheists. If anyone feels that the very word 'soul' already implies a religious outlook, substitute the word 'self' for the word 'soul' throughout this book. The word 'mind' is sometimes used in the sense in which I am using the word 'soul', as an individual thing, separate from the body; but 'mind' is often used in other senses, sometimes very unclear ones. For example, to say that someone has 'a good mind' may only mean that that person is intelligent, and may not in any way imply that the person has a part distinct from their body. Hence as far as possible I will avoid use of the noun 'mind'; and although I will use the adjective 'mental', I will give a precise definition in Chapter 2 of the sense in which I am using it.

Any philosophical argument which aims to reach clear and definite conclusions must define its crucial expressions. I put definitions of expressions which I use for the first time in bold type, so that when I use these expressions again at a later stage in the book, readers will be able easily to check what I mean by them. I have put a few of the more technical philosophical points which will be of interest only to those familiar with philosophical writing on the topic in endnotes and in the Appendix to Chapter 5, all of which may be ignored by others without losing the main points of my arguments.

B. The Problem of Personal Identity

It has always been of deep theoretical importance for our understanding of the world to know whether the world consists only of bits of matter or also of some things of a totally different kind from bits of matter, which interact with that matter. But it is also of great moral and practical importance to know what humans are. For surely the greater the difference between humans and machines, the more appropriate it is to treat them in very different ways from each other. Further, different views about the nature of human beings are closely connected to different views about the solution to the problem of personal identity. This is the problem of what it is for a person P_2 at time t_2 to be the same person as a certain person P_1 at an earlier time t_1. For example, what is it for a respectable citizen George in 2018 to be the same person as a 'George' who murdered someone in 1968? (Note that this is not, as such, a question about what it is for P_2 to have the same personality as P_1. Our personality is a matter of whether we are hard-hearted or kind, clever or stupid, knowledgeable or ignorant, impatient or patient. To say that someone's personality has changed is to say that he or she—one and the same person—had one personality at one time and a different personality at a different time. Our question is about what it is for P_2 to be the same person as P_1, whether or not he or she has the same personality.) If, as physicalism claims, we are merely physical substances, then whether the later George is the same person as the earlier 'George' depends on whether he is the same physical substance, and that can be spelled out in terms of whether he has the same body, or perhaps just the same brain, as the earlier George. 'Property dualism', a view intermediate between physicalism and substance dualism which I shall outline in Chapter 2, holds that humans have properties of two sharply different kinds—physical and mental. So it fits naturally with a view that, while the extent to which George has the same body or brain may play a major role in determining whether the later 'George' is the same person as the earlier George, this depends also on similarities between their 'mental' properties such as their beliefs, and chiefly on whether the memory beliefs of the later George about his past experiences coincide with the beliefs of the earlier George about his then current experiences. Substance dualism fits naturally with the view that whether the later George is the same person as the earlier George depends only on whether he has the same soul.

Most people normally suppose that, whichever of such philosophical views is correct, the later 'George' is in fact the same person as the earlier George iff the later George has the same body as the earlier George—at least as long as he seems to remember some of the experiences had by the earlier George. ('iff' means 'if and only if'.) But we cannot keep bodies under continuous observation; and so in the past we have used the later 'George''s appearance as evidence that the later 'George''s body is the same body as that of the earlier George. If he looks the same (or at least his appearance is different only in the kind of way that appearances change as people get older), then that (in the absence of evidence that George has an identical twin) is fairly good evidence that the later 'George''s body is the same body as that of the earlier George and so the later 'George' is the same person as the earlier George. Nowadays we can have much stronger evidence that two bodies are the same if their fingerprints and DNA are the same. More recently surgeons have learnt to transplant many bodily parts, and there is the serious possibility that very soon a surgeon will transplant a head. This raises the question whether the person with the transplanted head is the same person as the person who previously had the same body (apart from the head), or the same person as the person who previously had the head. We may well think that the essential part of a person's body is their brain, and so it is the person who has the brain of an earlier person who is that person. But it seems very probable that within the next few years neurosurgeons will be able to make large changes to a person's brain and to replace parts of it, and so to make great differences to that person's character and to what they seem to remember. (What a person seems to remember of what they did or experienced I shall often call their **memory beliefs or 'apparent memories', which I shall often shorten to 'a-memories'.** These may or may not be real memories; whether they are real memories depends on whether someone actually did or experienced those things and whether the person who seems to remember them was the person who actually did or experienced them.) When scientists do make changes such as I have described, then even if we know exactly what are the differences between the brain, apparent memories, and character of the earlier person and those of the later person, it will no longer be obvious whether the later person is or is not the same person as the earlier person. This is because there is no obvious answer to the question of how much of the body or brain or memory or character of the earlier person a later person needs to have in order to be the same person as that earlier person. If a large part of George's brain has been replaced by a part of a brain taken from another person, or neurosurgeons have radically altered George's a-memories, there will be a serious question about whether the later 'George' is the same person as the earlier George. A law court will need to know the answer to that question before they find the later 'George' guilty of some crime committed by the earlier George.

The same kind of question will arise for any person who has a serious brain disease which can be cured only by replacing a significant part of their brain, perhaps from the brain of a corpse in which that part is still capable of functioning. That person—let us call her 'Sally'—will want to know, before she agrees to have the operation, whether she is likely to survive the operation. Neurosurgeons are the experts who may be able to tell her whether after the operation Sally's body will be the body of a living, conscious person. They might even be able to predict how much about Sally's past that resulting person will seem to remember. But what their knowledge of neuroscience will not enable them to tell her is whether that post-operation person will be Sally or someone else (perhaps the person, part of whose brain was transplanted into Sally). This is because the issue is not about what the post-operation person will see or feel, or what their body or brain will be like, but about who that person is. Even if the scientists could predict with certainty exactly what would happen to all the atoms in the earlier Sally's brain, and exactly what the post-operation person would seem to remember, and what she would be like in every respect, their knowledge of neuroscience would not enable them to say whether that person would be the same person as the earlier Sally. And neither they nor the post-operation person would be in any better position after the operation to know whether the earlier Sally had survived. It is to be expected that the post-operation person would seem to have some of Sally's a-memories, but it is also to be expected that that person would seem to have some of the memories of the person from whose corpse the new brain part was taken. To begin to answer the all-important practical and moral question of who the post-operation person is, we need a view about what makes a person Sally. Is it just having a certain body, a certain brain (or a certain part of a brain), certain a-memories or character, or something rather different—having a certain soul? An answer to the question of what makes one person the same person as an earlier person will help us to answer the more general question about what persons are, and so what humans who are persons of a particular kind are. And that is what this book is about.

If and when we can answer these questions, we will be in a position to assess the plausibility of some of the procedures which 'transhumanists' are interested in performing in the more distant future. If scientists 'download' the whole contents of Sally's brain on to a computer, would that computer then be Sally? And if the content of George's brain was 'teletransported' into the brain of a person on a distant planet, would that person then be George? And this issue of what makes a person the same person as an earlier person has always been crucial in assessing the coherence of the claims of major religions that humans will live again on this earth or in another world after their death. In order to live again after their death, would someone need to have the same body, or at least the skull and bones of the earlier person? Or would it be enough if many of their a-memories about the actions and experiences of the earlier person are correct? Or would they need to have that person's soul? If someone's dead body is burnt to ashes in the crematorium, it is difficult to make sense of the notion that that very same body could exist again in a new afterlife; but there seems much less of a problem in supposing that—if humans have souls—their soul could continue to exist after the annihilation of their body, and perhaps be joined to a new body in an afterlife.

C. The Plan of This Book

I shall devote Chapter 2 to explaining some philosophical terms, and then—with the aid of these terms—to setting out and clarifying more fully the different theories about the nature of human beings. Then in Chapter 3 I shall proceed to a detailed discussion of theories of personal identity. These theories of personal identity can be divided into many complex theories and one simple theory. A '**complex theory of personal identity**' claims that 'being the same person' is analysable in terms of the later person having some of the same body or some of the same physical or mental properties as the earlier person—for example, having much of the same brain or many of the same memory beliefs as the earlier person—or some degree of continuity with the body or properties of the earlier person. What I mean by a later person having 'some degree of continuity with the body' of an earlier person is that their body is the result of gradual replacement of parts of the earlier body over time by new parts. And what I mean by a later person having 'properties with some degree of continuity with those of an earlier person' is that their properties are the result of gradual change over time to the properties of the earlier person. (For example, their physical properties—such as their weight and appearance—gradually change, and they gradually lose some of the memory beliefs of the earlier person while at the same time acquiring memory beliefs about events later than those experienced by the earlier person.) The **'simple theory of personal identity'** claims that 'being the same person' cannot be analysed in terms of having some of the same body or the same physical or mental properties (or any bodily parts or any physical or mental properties continuous with those of the earlier person); a later person might be the same person as an earlier person, whether or not he or she has any of the same body or the same physical or mental properties (or body or properties continuous with those of the earlier person). I shall conclude Chapter 3 by rejecting all complex theories and claim that the simple theory provides the only satisfactory theory of personal identity.

I shall then argue in Chapter 4 that it follows from a simple theory that there is a non-physical part of each person, our soul, which makes us who we are. The question then arises whether any body (and so brain) at all is necessary for our continuing existence. Could we continue to exist merely as disembodied souls? A famous argument due to the seventeenth-century French philosopher René Descartes claims that we could, and that our soul alone is sufficient for our continuing existence. By claiming that we 'could' exist without a body, he was claiming only that this is 'logically' possible; that is, that it would not involve a contradiction to suppose that we could exist without a body; he was not claiming that this is physically possible. This logical possibility, Descartes claims, has the consequence that each actually existing human is essentially a soul, an immaterial thing to which a body is attached while we are alive on earth.

Most thinkers of the Western (and Middle Eastern) world before the seventeenth century held that every human has a non-physical soul, but some of them held that he or she could not exist, or could not exist 'fully', without also having a body. I shall follow Descartes in defending the extreme version of a soul theory which claims that we are essentially souls, which are joined on earth to bodies; our thoughts and feelings and other mental events are ours because they are events in our souls. I do not wish to deny that—given the operation of the laws of nature which currently operate on earth—our souls are kept in existence by the operation of our brains, and that brain events cause many of the mental events in our souls. But my claim is that if those laws ceased to operate and so to bind body and soul together, it would be the continuing existence of our souls—if they continued to exist—which would constitute the continuing existence of us.

Almost without exception modern philosophers have claimed that Descartes's argument contains some simple error; and textbooks of the philosophy of mind often begin with a quick 'refutation' of his argument. I shall claim that although Descartes's original argument does not prove as much as he intended, a slightly amended version of it does prove all that he intended. However, there is a very powerful objection to Descartes's argument which, if it were cogent, would also defeat my amended version of the argument, as well as Descartes's original argument. This is the objection that Descartes's argument depends on a crucial assumption that when each of us refers to 'I', we know to what we are referring; we know what the 'I' is about which we are trying to assess the different theories. But that, the objection claims, is to beg the crucial question. I argue in Chapter 5 that this objection to Descartes's argument rests on ignoring an important philosophical distinction between what I call 'informative' and 'uninformative' designators, and I go on to explain how recognizing this distinction enables us to see the error involved in this powerful objection. I conclude that the simple theory of personal identity does indeed lead to the theory that each human being consists of two substances, body and soul, and that it is our soul which makes each of us who we are. Hence 'substance dualism'. I bring out that substance dualism is not merely a theory postulated as the best explanation of mental phenomena, but that our soul is a datum of experience. We are aware not merely of the occurrence of perceptions and thoughts, but also of ourselves as thinking and perceiving; and so, I argue, it is the 'I' of which each of us is aware in having any conscious experience which is our soul, the core of our identity; and it is the continued existence of our soul which constitutes the continued existence of each of us. I argue that the difference between any two souls is ultimate; they differ from each other without needing to have different mental properties (such as different thoughts or feelings)—they are just different from each other.

I then go on in Chapter 6 to defend the view that each person's soul interacts with their brain. It follows that the physical world, including our bodies and brains, is not a 'closed system'; not merely do our brains cause events in our souls, but we, that is our souls, cause events in our brains which cause us to move our limbs. I argue that any arguments by scientists purporting to establish the contrary, that is to establish 'the causal closure of the physical', would themselves depend for their justification on the assumption that the physical realm is not closed, and hence would be self-defeating. I come in Chapter 7 to consider whether there could be a scientific explanation of the origin of human souls and their interaction with brains and so with bodies. I claim that it is plausible to suppose that there is a law of nature which brings it about that at a certain stage of its development each human foetus gives rise to *a* connected soul. And certainly, there are also very many detailed laws of nature determining that brain events of particular types cause mental events of particular types in souls, and that mental events of particular types in souls cause brain events of particular types. For example, there is some law that a certain type of brain event caused by looking at a tree outside a window causes in the soul connected to it a visual image of a tree and a belief that there is a tree outside the window; and there is some law that a different type of brain event caused by the noise of a passing car causes a sound in the connected soul and a belief that a car is passing. And there is some law that an intention to move one's arm causes an event in the brain connected to it which—given that the brain is the brain of a typical healthy adult—normally causes their arm to move. However, in concluding Chapter 7, I shall argue that it is impossible—logically impossible and so impossible in any weaker sense—because of what a law of nature is that the operation of any law of nature could bring it about that a particular foetus gives rise to a particular soul. It is not possible that there is some law of nature which brings it about that your soul is connected to the brain to which it is in fact connected, and my soul is connected to the brain to which it is in fact connected, rather than vice versa.

2

Physicalism and Property Dualism

A. Human Beings

This book is about the nature of human beings. '**Human beings**' are persons belonging to the same biological group as ourselves; and that almost certainly involves having the same group of ancestors as ourselves. I understand by '**persons**' beings who have the capacity (or will have the capacity as a result of normal developmental processes) to have conscious events of certain kinds, including occurrent thoughts (thoughts which 'cross your mind') about past and future (such as 'John was born many years ago, and will soon be dead'), moral beliefs (beliefs about what is morally good and what is morally bad), and the ability to do some very simple logical reasoning (for example, to reason by mentally imaged symbols that 'if there are five apples in the bag, there are more than two apples in the bag'). By a '**conscious event**' I mean an experience of which the individual who has it is aware of having; a pain or an occurrent thought are conscious events because the individual who has them is aware of having them.[1] Hence when an organism has 'conscious events', there is what Thomas Nagel described as 'something it is like to be that organism'.[2] (Note that I do not mean by someone having 'conscious events' that they are awake, as opposed to being asleep or unaware of their surroundings. Someone who is asleep may be dreaming and so have conscious events of which they are aware.) I and my readers are not merely individuals who have the capacity to have conscious events, but persons. Human infants do not currently have the capacities to have moral beliefs or to do logical reasoning, but I am counting them—in accord with normal usage—as 'persons', because—given that they develop in the normal way—they will have those capacities in a few years' time. There may well be persons on distant planets, but they would not be human beings in the above biological sense. However, since most of the philosophical issues which I shall discuss have the same consequences for persons of all kinds, I ask the reader to assume— as I did in Chapter 1—that what I say about persons generally applies to humans, unless I specify otherwise.

B. Substances, Properties, and Events

Human beings are what philosophers call 'substances'. I shall under- stand by a **'substance'** a component of the world; a particular object or collection of objects. Thus my desk, the tree outside my window, the earth, the Milky Way, the photon (particle of light) emitted from a certain light source which landed on a certain screen, and each individual human being are all substances. Substances may have other substances as parts; my desk has as parts its drawers and the desk frame, and these too are substances. The world consists of all the substances that there are. Substances have properties. A **property may be an intrinsic property** of one substance, possessed by that substance quite independently of its relations to other substances; **or a relational property** consisting of a relation which a substance has to one or more other substances. Thus being square or brown, or having zero rest-mass, or growing larger or older, are intrinsic properties of substances. The window is square, and the photon has zero rest- mass. Being-to-the-left-of-the-cupboard or being-taller-than-James or moving-further-away-from-the-wall are relational properties of substances which relate them to other substances. The desk is to-the- left-of-the-cupboard, John is taller-than-James, and Sally is moving- further-away-from-the-wall. Substances exist and have properties for periods of time. My desk existed from 1920 when it was made, and will continue to exist until it is destroyed, maybe in 2030. Of the properties which a substance has, some are essential properties

(= logically necessary properties) of that substance. **An essential property of a substance** is one such that it is not logically possible for the substance to exist without having that property.

I must now explain these terms, 'logically necessary' and 'logically possible'. **A sentence s_1 is logically possible** iff it is not a contradiction and does not entail a contradiction. So a sentence is **logically impossible** iff it is a contradiction or entails a contradiction. **A sentence s_1 entails another sentence s_2 iff s_2 draws out something already implicit in s_1.** Thus 'Socrates is a human, and all humans are mortal' entails 'Socrates is mortal'. That some sentence s_1 entails another sentence is sometimes very obvious, but when this is not obvious you can often show it by producing a chain of entailments; that is, by showing that s_1 obviously entails some sentence s_{1a}, and s_{1a} obviously entails another sentence s_{1b}, and so on until you reach s_2; proofs in geometry or arithmetic draw out the more distant entailments of their premises. A contradiction is a sentence that has the form 'so-and-so and also not so-and-so'. Thus 'John was alive at 10am on 1 December 1920, and John was not alive at 10am on 1 December 1920' is a contradiction and so is obviously not logically possible. 'John killed his paternal grandmother before she could become pregnant for the first time' is not as it stands a contradiction, but it entails a contradiction, and you can prove that by drawing out the contradiction from it. For that sentence obviously entails 'The mother of John's father died before she could conceive a son or a daughter', and this latter sentence obviously entails 'The mother of John's father was not a mother', and that obviously entails 'There was someone who was not a mother, and also was a mother', which is a contradiction. Hence the original sentence is logically impossible because it entails a contradiction. So too does 'There is a male barber in a village who shaves all and only the men in the village who do not shave themselves'—I leave it to any reader unfamiliar with this apparently innocent sentence to work out why it entails a contradiction, and so is logically impossible.

I shall use **'conceivable'** in the same sense as 'logically possible'. So a sentence is 'conceivable'[3] iff either it is (was, or will be) true, or if the world had been different (in a way that does not entail a contradiction), it would have been true. And it is often obvious that some sentence is conceivable (= logically possible) without needing to try to prove it. A sentence is conceivable if one can understand what it would be like for it to be true—and if spelling out what it would be like for it to be true does not entail a contradiction. It is conceivable that 'no humans ever lived on earth', or that 'the world began to exist only 6,000 years ago'. Even though these sentences are false, they are 'conceivable' in the sense that they might have been true if the universe had begun in a different way, or if the laws of nature had been somewhat different from the actual laws of nature (that is, laws such as the laws of Quantum Theory or Relativity Theory); but it is not conceivable that there is a round square because that entails a contradiction—the world could never have been such that there exist round squares. So a sentence s_1 entails a sentence s_2 iff $\{s_1$ and not-$s_2\}$ is or entails a contradiction; {'Socrates is a human, and all humans are mortal' entails 'Socrates is mortal'} iff {'Socrates is a human, and all humans are mortal, but Socrates is not mortal'} entails a contradiction. A sentence is **logically necessary** iff its negation (the sentence which denies the former sentence) is not logically possible (= is logically impossible). Thus 'all squares have four sides' is logically necessary because it is not logically possible that 'there is a square which does not have four sides'. A sentence is **logically contingent** iff it is neither logically necessary nor logically impossible. Sentences express propositions. A **proposition** is what a sentence means. Two sentences which mean the same (= which make the same claim about how the world is), such as 'all humans are mortal', 'every human dies at some time', and 'tutti uomini sono mortali' (in Italian), express the same proposition. Because philosophers are concerned with what a sentence says rather than with the particular words or language it uses, I shall in future often talk about propositions rather than sentences. Then **a proposition is logically impossible/possible/necessary/contingent** iff any sentence which expresses it is logically impossible/possible/necessary/contingent.

It is important to distinguish the logically possible from the naturally possible and the practically possible. Not everything logically possible is naturally possible. **A proposition is naturally possible** iff the occurrence of what it asserts is compatible with the actual laws of nature (and, given that we are concerned with physical laws—that is, laws of nature about physical substances—such a proposition is **physically possible**). For example, although it is logically possible that something could travel faster than light, it is physically impossible that anyone could send a spaceship to a planet of another solar system at a velocity faster than the velocity of light (since the laws of Relativity Theory rule out anything travelling faster than light). It is, however, physically possible that humans could send such a spaceship at 99 per cent of the velocity of light. Whatever is entailed by the laws of nature is **naturally necessary** (and if these laws are physical laws, it is **physically necessary**); and whatever is incompatible with the laws of nature is **physically impossible** (and if these laws are physical laws, it is **physically impossible**). But not everything naturally possible is practically possible; that is, practically possible for humans now. **A proposition is practically possible** iff it is within the capacities of present-day humans to bring about now or in the foreseeable future what it asserts. It would take the research and development work of very many scientists, funded by a vast government grant over many decades, to send a spaceship to a planet of another solar system at 99 per cent of the velocity of light in the foreseeable future, and so it is not practically possible that NASA could send a spaceship to a planet of another solar system at 99 per cent of the velocity of light.

So—to repeat the definition—an essential property of a substance is one such that it is not logically possible that the substance could exist without that property. 'Occupying space' is an essential property of my desk; it is not logically possible that my desk could exist without occupying space. 'Being negatively charged' is an essential property of every electron; if an electron loses its negative charge, it ceases to exist. But some of the properties of a substance are non-essential (= 'logically contingent') properties of that substance; that is, it is logically possible that the substance could exist without that property. Being brown is a logically contingent property of my desk; if my desk were to be painted red instead of brown, the desk would still exist.

I define **an event** as some substance (or substances) either having (or gaining or losing) a certain property (or properties) at a certain time, or coming into existence or ceasing to exist at a certain time. Thus 'my desk being brown at 10am on 9 June 2008', 'Birmingham lying between Manchester and London during the whole twentieth century', and 'the birth of my mother in 1908' are events. In ordinary language it is normal to call only changes in some substance (or substances) 'events', while a substance having an unchanging property during some period of time is called a 'state' of that substance; and so only the desk being made in 1920 or the desk being destroyed in 2030 or ceasing to be owned by me, but not the desk being brown between 1920 and 2020, would count as 'events'. But it is useful to have a word covering all cases of substances having properties at times (as well as the comings into existence and ceasings to exist of substances); and, while sometimes also using the word 'state' in the ordinary sense, I shall use the word 'event' in this wide sense.

The different views on the issues to be discussed in this book are often expressed as claims about two substances or two properties or two events being the same substance, property, or event. Someone may claim that really a human being is just the same as—that is, the same substance as—his or her body, or that feeling pain just is having one's C-fibres (certain bundles of nerve cells) 'firing' (= emitting an electric discharge), and that me believing that $2+2=4$ just is the existence of certain connections between the neurons (nerve cells) in my brain. But in order to assess such claims, we need a view about what it is for two substances, properties, or events to be the same substance, property, or event—that is, we need criteria for what it is for one substance (property or event) picked out by one word to be the same substance as a substance (property or event) picked out by a different word, either at the same time or at a different time. Although 'substance' is a philosophers' technical term, the account which I have given earlier of what it is for something to be a substance makes it clear, as almost all philosophers would agree, that **there are different criteria of identity for substances of different kinds**. For example, being the same lump of bronze consists in being formed of (approximately) the same molecules. The lump of bronze about which I was talking' is the same lump of bronze as 'the lump of bronze about which you were talking' iff the two lumps of bronze are made of (approximately) the same molecules. Whereas being the same tree is having the same trunk and the same upper roots directly connected to the trunk; but having the same branches as the earlier tree is not in any way necessary for the tree to be the same tree. The question with which we shall be concerned in Chapter 3 is what it is for a person at one time to be the same person as a person at a later time.

There are no clear criteria in ordinary language of what it is for two properties or events to be the same property or event. Is the property of reflecting light of such-and-such a wavelength the same property as the property of being red, or are these different properties? Is the event of Brutus killing Caesar on the Ides of March the same event as Brutus stabbing Caesar on the Ides of March, or are these different events? Our inability to give easy answers to these questions is not due to there being some deep metaphysical truth about these matters which we have not been able to discover, but simply because we use the expressions 'same property' and 'same event' without there being clear criteria for what counts as the 'same property' and 'same event'. So if we are to use these expressions to express different philosophical views, we need sharp definitions of what it is for two properties or two events to be the same; and different philosophers offer different definitions. I now define **a property A as the same property as a property B** iff having A (of logical necessity) always makes the same difference to a substance as does having B, and vice versa.[4] On this definition the property of being a trilateral (being a closed three-sided rectilinear figure) is the same property as the property of being triangular (being a closed rectilinear figure having three internal angles)—because of logical necessity any triangle is trilateral, and conversely. The property of killing someone is the same property as the property of causing someone to die, but it is not the same property as stabbing someone, because you could kill someone without stabbing them. And the property of reflecting light of such-and-such a wavelength is not the same property as the property of being red, because—it is logically possible—something could be red without reflecting light of that wavelength. This is because the criteria for a substance being red are that it looks to most people to be of the same colour as such paradigm objects as ripe tomatoes, raspberries, London buses, or British post boxes, and it is not logically necessary that substances which reflect light of a certain wavelength look that way to most people—it's logically possible that in some other world they don't. Properties are what philosophers call 'universals'; that is, the same property may be had by many different substances; and there are properties which perhaps no substance will ever have—such as the property of being a trillion trillion years old.

By contrast, events are particular occurrences in the history of the world. I define **an event F as the same event as an event G** iff the occurrence of F makes (has made, or will make) the same difference to the actual world as does the occurrence of E. The normal case of two events being the same event is where they involve the same substance(s) (whether or not the substances are picked out by logically equivalent expressions), the same property, and the same time (with 'same property' defined in the way just defined). So, because 'London' and 'The 2018 capital of the UK' refer to the same city in the actual world (although 'London' and 'The 2018 capital of the UK' are not logically equivalent to each other), and being over-populated always (of logical necessity) makes the same difference to any substance as does having too large a population, 'London being overpopulated in 2018' and 'The 2018 capital of the UK having too large a population in 2018' are the same event.[5]

The point of defining 'same event' and so 'same property' in these ways is that on these definitions there is no more to the history of the world or to the history of some narrow spatiotemporal region of the world (in the objective sense of what has happened, is happening, or will happen) than all the events which have occurred, are occurring, or will occur in it or in that region. That history consists of each substance coming into existence at a certain time, acquiring or losing intrinsic properties, acquiring or losing relations to other substances, and then ceasing to exist at a certain time. It includes, for example, a particular desk being made, being painted brown, being placed 10ft. away from the wall, being moved 15ft. away from the wall, damaging the floor when moved, and then being destroyed. And so on for every substance. If you listed all the events which are different from each other on my definition, there would be nothing more to the history of the world or some narrow spatiotemporal region of it than what is listed there.

Finally, I need to define a philosophical term much used in discussions of our topic—'**supervenient**'. Properties are said to 'supervene' on other properties, and events are said to 'supervene' on other events. To say that some property A 'supervenes' on another property B can mean simply that a substance having B causes the substance to have A, and to say that some event of a substance having A 'supervenes' on another event of that substance having B can mean merely that the second event causes the first event. However, in discussions of the topic of this book, 'supervenes' is not normally used in that causal sense. In philosophical writing about the topic of this book 'supervenes' is normally understood in a much stronger sense, as follows. **A property A supervenes on a property B** iff (of logical necessity) any event of a substance having the property A would (if it occurred) make no further difference to the world additional to that made by an event of that substance having the property B, but the event of a substance having B would make a further difference to the world additional to the event of that substance having A; and any substance which has B has A because it has B.[6] So having B involves having A, but having A does not involve having B. Thus being 'coloured' supervenes on being 'green', because any substance being coloured is nothing extra beyond it being green, but it being green is something extra beyond it being coloured; and substances are coloured because they are green (and not vice versa). **An event F supervenes on an event E** iff (of logical necessity) the occurrence of F makes no further difference to the actual world beyond the occurrence of E, but the occurrence of E does make a further difference beyond the occurrence of F; and F occurs because E occurs. So 'my desk being symmetrical at 10am' supervenes on 'my desk being square at 10am'; the desk being symmetrical is not something further beyond it being square. Rather, the desk being symmetrical is already involved in it being square, but it being square is something extra beyond it being symmetrical; and it is symmetrical because it is square (and not vice versa). As the point is sometimes expressed, God would not need to do anything extra beyond making my desk square in order to make it symmetrical, but he could make it symmetrical without making it square.

C. Physicalism

I can now use these definitions to articulate the different views about the nature of human beings in a more precise way than I was able to do in Chapter 1. I begin by discussing views rival to my own, the most extreme of which is **physicalism**. I understand physicalism as the doctrine that humans are physical substances, and that all the properties of humans are physical properties or properties supervening on these.[7] I shall **provisionally understand by a physical substance** a substance, all of whose essential properties are physical properties or properties supervenient on physical properties. I shall **provisionally understand by a physical property** a property of a kind possessed by inanimate substances, as well as often by humans and higher animals, or a conjunction or disjunction of such properties. (A **conjunction** of several properties P, Q, R is the property 'P and Q and R'. A **disjunction** of several properties P, Q, R is the property 'P or Q or R'.) So both properties such as having a certain mass or electric charge possessed by fundamental particles like electrons and protons, and properties possessed by larger inanimate substances composed of fundamental particles, such as being slippery or octagonal, or flat or mountainous, are physical properties. Thus a particular table is a physical substance, since the essential properties of such a table are being made of such-and-such solid matter (for example, wood or steel), having a flat surface, having a certain height, and being used by humans for putting things on. All of these properties are typical physical properties. Among other physical substances are gates,

roads, trees, and other plants. Also, human bodies are physical substances, because their only essential properties are properties of
height, mass, and having as parts a brain and most other typical
human organs such as a heart, liver, and limbs interacting in certain
ways. The parts of our bodies, such as our brains, are also physical
substances; the essential properties of human brains include such
properties as consisting of a cerebrum and cerebellum, interconnected by complicated neural networks of certain kinds. But physicalism claims not merely that human bodies or brains are physical
substances, but that humans themselves are physical substances,
since—it holds—all their essential properties are physical properties
(or properties supervenient on physical properties). I shall **provisionally understand by a physical event** an event of a substance having a
physical property (or gaining or losing a physical property) at a
particular time, or a physical substance coming into existence or
ceasing to exist at a particular time. Among physical events are events
in a human brain, such as neurons firing.

Clearly, however, humans have, as well as physical properties,
properties which inanimate substances do not have; humans get
angry, are in pain, are afraid, intend to go to London, believe that
the world is very old, have thoughts about philosophy, and so on; and
tables and planets, electrons and protons, do not have these properties. **I shall provisionally understand by a mental property** a property of this kind which humans (and the higher animals) have, but
physical substances do not have. I shall understand by a **mental
substance** (if there are any such) a substance which has at least one
essential mental property (whether or not it also has any essential
physical properties). **Mental events** are events of a substance having
(or gaining or losing) a mental property (or a mental substance
coming into existence or ceasing to exist) at a particular time.
Among mental events are such events as 'James being angry with
John all last week' and 'George being in pain on 22 October 2017'.

Physicalists claim that all mental properties are really identical to
physical properties or supervene on them, and that that is why all
humans are physical substances; and that all mental events are really

identical to physical events or supervene on them. Different versions of physicalism give different accounts of what makes it the case that mental properties are the same as, or supervene on, physical properties. On some versions of physicalism the properties are identical because the predicates denoting the properties (= the words which refer to the properties) have the same meaning as combinations of words denoting physical properties. For example, '**analytical behaviourism**' holds that to have a mental property just is to behave in a way which can be analysed in terms of the publicly observable movements of our limbs, tongue, and other bodily organs, movements of kinds which inanimate objects also make. According to analytical behaviourism, 'James is angry with John' means something like: 'James said that John had hurt him, and so hit John and/or did not talk to or shake hands with John in circumstances where he would normally do this, and so on'. The analytical behaviourist will admit that 'said that John had hurt him' needs to be spelled out more fully in physical terms; and the 'and so on', as a full analysis of 'being angry' in terms of public behaviour, would need to be a long and complicated disjunction of conjunctions of physical events. But the behaviourist claims that such an analysis could be provided. Yet, contrary to analytical behaviourism, it seems obvious that people may be angry without this ever being shown by their public behaviour. One physicalist theory which seeks to take account of this point is called '**analytical functionalism**'. This theory holds that having a mental property is to be analysed as having an internal bodily state (in particular, a brain state) which is *normally* caused in a certain kind of way and *tends* to cause a certain pattern of behaviour. 'James is angry with John' just means something like 'James has an internal state of a kind normally caused by such publicly observable causes as being hurt by someone's conduct, and which tends to cause behaviour [of the kind just described above]'. Analytical functionalism differs from analytical behaviourism in that for functionalism, being angry consists in having a certain internal state; and that internal state is not always caused in the same way and will not always cause any public behaviour—it is simply the state that is *normally* caused in a certain way and *tends* to cause similar behaviour and so normally does cause it.

However, it does seem fairly evident that expressions denoting mental properties do not mean the same as any expressions denoting physical properties. 'James is angry with John' does not *mean* the same as—is not *synonymous with*—some assertion describing his behaviour or the physical events causing or caused by some internal state of his, even if normally whenever James is angry with John, he behaves in a certain way or has a brain state of a certain kind. To say that James is angry is to say something about his thoughts and feelings, not about his behaviour or his brain states which cause that behaviour or are caused by the behaviour of other people. So many contemporary physicalists adopt a theory called '**type-type identity theory**'. This claims that mental events are physical events, not because the expressions denoting mental properties mean the same as expressions denoting physical properties, but because empirical science has shown (or is almost certainly on the way to showing) that whenever any person has a particular mental property, that person always has a particular brain property, and vice versa. Thus it might be the case that whenever humans are in pain, their C-fibres fire, and a human's C-fibres never fire without that human being in pain. Similarly, the theory claims that whenever some human is angry, their brain is in one type of state; and whenever some human's brain is in that type of state, that human is angry. And so on. Hence, the theory boldly concludes, a human having a certain mental property just is that human having a certain brain property, and so the mental property is the same property as the brain property and the mental event of some particular human having that property is the same event as the physical event of that human having the brain property. So (because all mental properties are physical properties) all the properties of any human are physical properties, and so humans are physical substances.

Type-type identity theory certainly seems to violate the account of what it is for one event to be the same as another event, which I provided in the previous section. For a human being in pain seems to make a further difference to the world from the mere occurrence of some event in his or her brain, and it would therefore seem to give a more adequate account of what is happening to say that two events are occurring—a brain event and a pain—such that an occurrence of an event of the one kind is correlated with the occurrence of an event of the other kind. But even if we suppose for the moment that the identity of one property with another, and the identity of one event with another, is to be established by the existence of invariable one-one correlations between them, there is a major problem with type-type identity theory that it is rather unlikely that there are such one-one correlations between the two types of events. This is the problem of 'multiple realizability'. Physicalists, like most of us, believe—surely correctly—that higher animals such as dogs and cats whose brains are very similar to ours, and perhaps birds and fish whose brains are somewhat different from ours, and also just possibly persons on distant planets with very different kinds of brains from those of humans (if there are any such persons), also have mental events. But it is at least logically possible that some beings who have mental events of some type—for example, feeling pain—do not have a brain event of the same type as we do when we have a mental event of that type—for example, as we do when we feel pain. Pains in fish may be correlated with different events in their brains from the events with which pains in humans are correlated. So the property of being in pain cannot be the same property as any one physical property, since someone could be in pain without being in the same brain state as we are when we are in pain. Physicalism can meet this difficulty by claiming merely that no conscious being ever has a mental event of some type without there being a brain event (or some other physical event) of one of many particular types correlated with it, and that the mental event occurs because of the brain event (and not vice versa). Thus it might be that whenever humans are in pain, their C-fibres fire; but whenever fish are in pain (if they do feel pain), their C-fibres do not fire (some species of fish do not even have C-fibres) but a brain event (or other physical event) of some different type occurs—for example, their A-delta fibres fire; and whenever the A-delta fibres of a fish fire, the fish is in pain. And for organisms of different kinds, perhaps to be found on distant planets, such organisms being in pain might be correlated with types of event in those organisms' bodies totally unknown to us.

So in the face of the problem of 'multiple realizability', physicalists typically modify their claim of identity between mental and physical properties (and mental and physical events) to a claim of supervenience. **Mind-brain supervenience theory** assumes that whenever any mental event occurs (for example, some organism has a pain), there occurs a brain event of some type (for example, that organism's C-fibres or A-delta fibres fire), such that the occurrence of any brain event of that type is correlated with a mental event of the former type, and that the mental event (the pain) could not fail to occur if the correlated brain event occurs; but the brain event occurs because of the occurrence of other physical events. Given that assumption, the theory holds the occurrence of every mental event is involved in the occurrence of some brain event, and so when the brain event occurs, the mental event occurs, and so the mental event is nothing extra beyond the occurrence of the brain event. But what makes mind-brain supervenience theory different from type-type identity theory is that—according to mind-brain supervenience theory—the occurrence of a mental event of a certain type (for example, a pain) need not be involved in the occurrence of a physical event only of one particular type, but merely in the occurrence of a physical event of some type or other. So the mental property supervenes on the physical property, and the mental event supervenes on the physical event. (Another way used to make the same claim is to say that the mental event is 'realized by' the brain event—hence the description of the problem which gives rise to this theory as the problem of 'multiple realizability'.)

As an instance of one physical event supervening on another physical event, the American philosopher David Lewis gave the example of a dot-matrix picture, in which a pattern of dots forms a picture of a face.[8] All there is to the picture is dots or empty spaces without dots at each point of the matrix. Yet many different arrangements of dots would produce the same picture. (You would recognize the same face in many different arrangements of the dots.) Analogously, claims the mind-brain supervenience theorist, there is nothing more to the occurrence of any mental event additional to the occurrence of a brain event, and yet the same type of mental event could be involved in different types of brain events. All the versions of physicalism considered previously are sometimes called 'reductive physicalist theories' because they 'reduce' all mental properties and events to physical ones. By contrast, the supervenience theory is often called a 'non-reductive' physicalist theory, because it claims that mental properties and events are not the same as physical properties and events. It is, however, 'reductive' in claiming that all mental properties and events are involved in physical properties and events in the sense described previously. If this theory were true, there would be no more to the history of the world than physical events. So if you knew all the physical events (in the senses of 'physical' and 'event' which I have defined), you could work out by armchair reasoning, without doing any more experiments or taking into account any other evidence, which mental events had occurred.

But surely, on the contrary, however much you knew about some person's brain and other physical events, that would not prove conclusively what the person was thinking or feeling. It is logically possible, there is no contradiction in supposing, that on some occasion the correlations between types of brain event and types of mental event which normally hold did not hold; and so that some brain event occurred without a mental event of the type normally correlated with it occurring. Just once some person might have a brain event of a kind normally correlated with having a pain without that person having a pain on that occasion. And in fact the occurrence of any particular brain event never entails even that any mental event at all is occurring, let alone which one—although of course the occurrence of some particular brain event together with information that brain events of that type have been correlated in the past with mental events of a certain type provides strong evidence (= makes it very probable) that a mental event of a certain type is occurring. More generally, if a traveller from another planet where there are persons with bodies of quite different kinds from any bodies found on earth visited earth, he could learn everything about human bodies and brains, and note that humans scream if you stick knives into them; but, however clever he was in working out the consequences of what he had discovered, he could still rationally wonder whether humans are simply inanimate machines programmed to scream whenever a knife is stuck into them, or whether they scream because they are in pain, and more generally whether they have feelings. It would still be consistent with whatever the traveller discovered about their bodies and brains to hold that humans are never conscious—what he holds does not entail a contradiction. The relation of the dot-matrix to the picture it produces is very different from the relation of a brain event to its correlated mental event, because there *is* a contradiction in supposing that the same pattern of dots which in fact produces the picture could occur without producing the picture; but there is not a contradiction in supposing that—even if we suppose that everything else in the world remains the same—a certain brain event could have occurred without the occurrence of any mental event of a type normally correlated with it. I conclude that mental events are extra events in the history of the world additional to brain events and other physical events. Mental properties are not identical to physical properties, nor do they supervene on them; and mental events are not identical to physical events, nor do they supervene on them.

D. Property Dualism

While I believe that the conclusion in the last sentence follows from the simple argument given in the previous paragraph, that conclusion becomes even more obvious when we examine the source of the distinction between mental and physical events. I followed most philosophical discussions by defining physical properties as ones of a kind possessed by inanimate substances as well as by humans and higher animals (or conjunctions or disjunctions thereof), and phys-ical events and substances as ones which involve physical properties in a specified way; and I defined mental properties as ones possessed only by humans and the higher animals and not by inanimate substances, and mental events and substances as ones which involve mental properties in a specified way. But, while this way of distinguishing the mental from the physical enables us to see the kinds of events and properties which belong to each group, it does not bring out why it is that inanimate substances do not and humans and higher animals do have mental properties.

I suggest that what underlies this superficial difference is a fundamental distinction between events of two kinds, from which the distinction between properties can be derived. What is common to all the events which humans and higher animals have and inanimate objects do not have is that the former can be experienced only by their subject; that is, the human or animal involved in them. What makes an event a 'mental event' is that it is an event to which the substance involved in the event has privileged access by experiencing it. That is what makes pains and thoughts and the intentions which we are trying to fulfil mental events. Whatever ways others have of finding out whether I am seeing the tree outside my window or have a thought that today is Thursday or am intending to shut the door, I could also use; like others, I could study my behaviour by watching a film of it, or inspect my brain via some instrument. But I have an additional way of finding out whether I am seeing the tree or have the thought that today is Thursday or am intending to shut the door, by actually having the experience of seeing the tree or having the thought or intention; and no one else could have that way of knowing about these events. That is what makes these events mental events. A mental event would not be my mental event unless I could become aware of it by experiencing it. And since an event is the event it is partly in virtue of the substance (such as a human) who has it, no one else can have my mental events. Someone else can have a pain of the same intensity and duration at the same time as I do, but there would be two different pains—her pain and my pain.

By contrast, what makes it the case that inanimate objects as well as humans and higher animals have physical events is that they are public events. What makes an event a physical event is that it is an event to which no one substance can have privileged access by experiencing it. Any physical event is necessarily equally accessible to any human with the right training. It is for this reason that all the events which happen in the inanimate world and also all the events in our bodies are physical events. A brain event—a certain neuron 'firing' at a certain time—is a physical event; although it may cause someone to have a sensation, the brain event is not itself an event to which anyone has the unique access of the kind they have to their sensations. Any human suitably located, with faculties in working order (such as having normal sight), equipped with the necessary instruments and trained to recognize brain events, can find out about your brain events as well as you can. This way of making the distinction between the physical and the mental will classify the same events and properties as 'physical' and 'mental', as did the earlier account, but it explains why humans and higher animals have properties of a kind which inanimate substances do not have. So in future I will use **revised definitions of 'a mental event'** as 'an event to which there is privileged access by the substance involved in the event experiencing it', and **a 'physical event'** as an 'an event to which no one substance can have privileged access by experiencing it'.

I now define a **'pure mental event'** as one whose occurrence does not involve the occurrence of any physical event; its occurrence is compatible with the occurrence of any particular brain or other physical event, or no physical event at all. While me-seeing-a-tree is a mental event, because necessarily I have privileged access to what I am seeing by actually having the experience of seeing it, me-seeing-a-tree is not a 'pure mental event' since its occurrence involves the existence of a tree which is a physical event. I wouldn't count as 'seeing' the tree unless there is a tree which is reflecting light rays which cause me to be aware of it. But me-seeming-to-see-a-tree is a pure mental event, because it could seem to me that I am seeing a tree without any tree existing, or without the occurrence of any other particular physical event. There is no contradiction involved in supposing that just once in human history it-seemed-to-someone-that-they-are-seeing-a-tree   without   there being any cause at all of that event. No one could discover what causes it-to-seem-to-someone-that-they-are-seeing-a-tree merely by examining how it seemed, and so it is not involved in me-seeming-to-see-a-tree that some particular brain event or any particular physical event at all occurs. You need to study what happens in the brain in order to discover what causes me-seeming-to-see-a-tree, or whether—improbably—that it has no cause. I'll call a mental event which does involve a physical event an 'impure mental event'.

It follows directly from my definitions that no mental event is a physical event, and no mental event 'supervenes on' a physical event (in the sense described earlier). For on my definitions a 'mental event' is an event to which the substance involved in the event has privileged access by experiencing it, and a 'physical event' is one to which no substance has privileged access by experiencing it. And although some mental events, the impure mental events, involve physical events, no physical event involves a mental event, for no event to which there is no privileged access could involve an event to which there is privileged access.

Revised definitions of 'physical property' and 'mental property' follow naturally from the revised definitions of mental and physical events. I shall call any property which (of logical necessity) always makes the event of a substance having that property a mental event a **mental property**; and any property which (of logical necessity) always makes an event of a substance having that property a pure mental event a **pure mental property**; and I shall call any property which (of logical necessity) always makes an event of a substance having that property a physical event a **physical property**. So the property of seeing a tree is a mental property, the property of thinking about philosophy is a pure mental property, and the property of having a mass of 10kg is a physical property. The earlier definition of a **physical substance** as a substance, all of whose essential properties are physical properties (or properties supervenient on physical properties), can now be understood as concerned with physical properties in the sense just defined. Thus any individual electron is a physical substance because it is an electron in virtue of having the properties of having a certain mass and a certain electric charge, and it is the particular electron it is in virtue of having the property of having a certain spatial location at a certain time.[9] Likewise, all medium-sized substances composed only of fundamental particles are also physical substances. The house which I own is a physical substance because what makes that house a house is that it is a building made of solid material, used by a small group of humans as the place where they meet and eat. It is the particular house which it is because of its shape and size and location, and because it has the property of being made largely of certain particular bricks. Anyone can find out that a substance has these properties as well as can anyone else, and so they are physical properties. Since these are the only properties needed for my house to be that house (= the only essential properties of that house), that house is a physical substance. The earlier definition of a **mental substance** as a substance which has a mental property as one of its essential properties will now be understood as concerned with a mental property in the sense just defined. I shall come on shortly to discuss whether humans are mental substances in this sense.

The point of my adopting my particular definitions of 'physical' and 'mental' property, substance, and event is that they 'carve reality at the joints'; that is, they bring out sharp distinctions between very different kinds of things in the world of immense importance for understanding what there is in the world and how we interact with the world. The earlier discussion reached the conclusion that we have not merely mental events, but pure mental events; that is, events which do not involve any physical events. That there are events of two different kinds, which I am calling 'physical events' and 'pure mental events', neither of which involve the other, each normally[10] involving a property of one of two different kinds, is the theory which, following normal usage, I shall call **'property dualism'**. Physical events often cause pure mental events, and it seems that pure mental events (for example, our intentions) often cause physical events (brain events and thereby our bodily movements). The history of each human consists of both their pure mental events and their physical events.

E. The Different Kinds of Pure Mental Events

I shall be concerned in future almost entirely with pure mental properties and events, and so I ask the reader to assume—even if I do not say this explicitly—that all my references in future to 'mental properties' or 'mental events' are references to 'pure mental properties' and 'pure mental events' unless I specify otherwise. There are, I suggest, several different kinds of pure mental events. My arguments so far have been concerned mainly with just one kind of pure mental event—pains; but what I have written about pains applies to sensations of other kinds. **Sensations** include not merely pains and other feelings, but also patterns of colour in a visual field, sounds, tastes and smells as sensed by the person whose they are, and the ways in which physical things seem, look, and feel to some person. These events are mental because the substance involved (the person whose they are) has privileged access to them by experiencing them; and—since their occurrence does not involve the occurrence of any physical event— they are pure mental events. Such events are of course normally caused by brain events; but brain events are different events from sensations. The occurrence of a sensation as such never involves the occurrence of a brain event, since there is no contradiction involved in supposing that on some occasion our world could be different in the sole respect that some sensation occurred uncaused by any brain event. Nor does the occurrence of any brain event ever involve the occurrence of a sensation. However much a visitor from another planet knew about our brains, that would be compatible either with the occurrence or with the non-occurrence of sensations in us.

Among pure mental events, I shall now argue, there are—in addition to sensations—beliefs, thoughts, intentions (= purposes), and desires. We have innumerable **beliefs** about big and small matters. We may believe that there is food in the cupboard, that bread nourishes and that toadstools poison, that the universe is many billions of years old, or that there is a God. By **'thoughts'** I mean occurrent thoughts, thoughts that occur at particular times, and which we may or may not believe. The thought that today is

Thursday, or that I am old, 'crosses my mind' at a particular time. And then we have **intentions**. By an intentional action I mean an action which an agent does, meaning to do it. And so when an agent performs or tries to perform some intentional action, they have an intention (= purpose) in what they are doing or trying to do. The intention may be an intention to do an action which takes many minutes, for example to walk to the railway station. Each of the bodily movements which I make in executing that intention are intentional actions, but there is only one intention which guides them—my body executes that intention for me. We seem to guide our intentional actions by our intentions. And when we try to do some action but do not succeed, for example when I try to untie a knot but fail because the knot is too tight, we still had the intention to untie the knot.

I distinguish short-term intentions from long-term intentions. I understand by a short-term intention one by which at the time when someone has it, they are trying to make a difference to the world at that time (normally by means of the movements of their body, but sometimes merely by forcing themselves to think about some topic). For example, if I utter a sentence, meaning to do so (that is, I utter it intentionally), or walk to the railway station, I am executing a short-term intention to utter that sentence or walk to the station. Many of the intentional actions we do each day—for example, the sequence of actions we perform in dressing or going to work each morning—we do out of habit; and so we form and are guided by the intention to do each of these actions out of habit. But sometimes we form a new intention, for example to walk to work by a different route, and forming a new intention is a decision. Our decisions are much more to the forefront of our consciousness than are our habitual intentions.

I understand by a long-term intention one by which someone tries to guide their short-term intentions when it is relevant to them. For example, if I have a long-term intention to lose weight, that influences me to try to form short-term intentions to eat or not to eat this or that at various times. But some of the time I do not have the opportunity to choose whether to eat or not to eat, and then the long-term intention makes no difference to what I try to do. (I shall assume, until we reach Chapter 6, that things are as they seem in this respect: that our intentions which seem to influence our bodily movements do in fact do so. However, a considerable number of philosophers and scientists claim that this is an illusion, and that our intentions make no difference to our bodily movements. I shall discuss and reject this claim in Chapter 6.)

Many of our actions are consequences of forming intentions which we are influenced to form by our **desires**, in the sense of felt inclinations to do this or that—for example, to eat the cake, to kick the table or the man who insulted me, or to go to bed. We can, however, resist our desires and not allow them to influence our behaviour. (I suggest that all pure mental events can be analysed in terms of mental events of the kinds so far described. For example, 'being angry' can be analysed in terms of a conjunction of a belief (such as the belief that someone or something has hurt you), a desire (such as the desire to hurt someone or something), and a sensation (such as a tight feeling in the stomach). But nothing in my argument turns on this; there may well be pure mental events of kinds which cannot be analysed in such ways.)

It is evident that each human has privileged access by experience to their (occurrent) thoughts as well as to their sensations. No brain event or other public event involves me having the thought 'crossing my mind' that today is Thursday, nor does the occurrence of that thought involve any brain event. Many philosophers who admit that sensations (and maybe thoughts) are pure mental events hold that someone having some belief, or having some intention in what they are doing, or some desire to do some action, is simply a matter of the way they behave publicly. But that is not so. Beliefs by themselves have no consequences for public behaviour, and neither do intentions or desires by themselves. Beliefs only lead to public behaviour if combined with intentions; and different combinations of beliefs and intentions may lead to the same public behaviour. You have a headache, you ask me for an aspirin, I give you a pill; it is a poison pill and you die. My action may be the result of a belief that the pill was an aspirin and my intention to cure your headache; or the result of a belief that the pill was poisonous and my intention to kill you. And the combination of a belief and an intention only leads to public behaviour if our limbs or tongue or other organs are working properly. If I am suddenly incapacitated, no public action will occur. Of course we can often make very probably correct inferences from someone's past behaviour and publicly observable history to the intentions and beliefs which it is most probable they have; but that is compatible with them suddenly forming a new intention (e.g. to kill someone), and clearly the person who has the intention has a means of access not available to any other human to whether he has that intention and so whether he has the requisite belief.

Most of our intentions require some belief about how to execute them—as in the example just discussed—and so by themselves have no consequences for public behaviour. But some of our intentions are merely intentions to move some bodily part such as a limb; and in these cases our intentions can cause the movement without us needing a belief about how to do this. Yet in these cases also we can have an intention to move a limb which does not cause the limb to move because we find ourselves incapacitated; and bodily movements of a kind which are normally caused by intentions can occur without being caused by an intention. Football referees faced with evidence that one player's leg movement caused an opposing player to fall over have to reach a verdict about whether the former player had the intention of causing the opponent's fall. They may reach a probable conclusion on the basis of what they see, but necessarily the player has a means of access not available to the referee to whether he had the intention of tripping up his opponent. Likewise someone can have **desires**, for example to smoke a cigarette or eat chocolate, to which they never yield or tell anyone about; and they know by experiencing it better than anyone else does whether they have that desire.

Thoughts, beliefs, intentions, and desires are all what I shall call **'propositional events'**,[11] meaning by that that they all involve an attitude to some possible event which can be expressed by a proposition, that is in a sentence: a desire or intention to bring such an event about, or a thought or belief that such an event has occurred, is occurring, or will occur. Thoughts and short-term intentions, like sensations, are **conscious events**, in the sense that their occurrence entails that the subject is to some degree aware that they are occurring. It would make no sense to suppose that some thought was 'crossing your mind' without you being aware that it is crossing your mind. Nor can you have a short-term intention without being aware that you are guiding your behaviour by it. By contrast, beliefs and desires and long-term intentions are **continuing mental events**, in the sense that they continue to exist while the subject is not conscious of them; the subject's privileged access to them at any time depends on her ability to bring them then to consciousness by introspection, by asking herself whether she has the particular desire or belief or long-term intention. I have innumerable beliefs, many desires, and some long-term intentions of which I am not currently conscious—for example, beliefs about history or geography, desires to meet or not meet certain people, or intentions to write a book or to be more agreeable to colleagues; but I can bring these beliefs, desires, and intentions to consciousness by asking myself what do I believe about so-and-so, what do I desire to happen in some respect, and what am I trying to achieve by some of my behaviour.

That some person has privileged access to some belief by being able to experience having it is what makes that belief his or hers. There are, however, some **subconscious beliefs** in the sense of beliefs which we refuse to admit to ourselves that we have. A person may refuse to admit to themself that they believe that their husband has been unfaithful or that their daughter has committed a crime. In these cases it may need help from others, sometimes including psychiatrists, to make them aware of their beliefs. But among principles which influence our conduct, there is a sharp distinction between, on the one hand, those by which we are consciously or subconsciously guiding our conduct and so are such that if we make enough effort to be honest with ourselves we can bring them to consciousness, and, on the other hand, those principles which are such that, however hard we try, we cannot bring them to consciousness; and so there is good reason to confine the word 'belief' so that this applies only to the former. If—as most of us believe—computers are not conscious, they don't have 'beliefs'; they are just guided by principles built into them by others. Hence it remains the case that we do have privileged access to our subconscious beliefs by experiencing them, a kind of access which others cannot have. And just as there are subconscious beliefs, so also there are **subconscious intentions and desires,** ones which we can bring to consciousness if we make enough effort to be honest with ourselves, an effort for which we may need help from others.

F. Physical and Mental Substances

I defined property dualism as the theory that—contrary to physicalism—there are events of two different kinds, which I am calling 'physical events' and 'pure mental events', neither of which involve the other, each normally involving a property of one of two different kinds; pure mental events are not the same as, nor do they supervene on, physical events. What I shall call **mere property dualism** differs from physicalism only in these respects. A crucial difference between mere property dualism and other theories which I shall be discussing later in this book is that it holds, as does physicalism, that humans are physical substances. I defined a substance as a physical substance iff all its essential properties are physical properties. So, to repeat the point, the particular body which is mine is a physical substance. It is a body because of its shape, and its limbs and organs (arms, legs, lungs, heart, brain, etc.) being interconnected in certain characteristic ways. It is the particular body it is because most of its parts are made from certain particular cells, or cells resulting from the gradual replacement of those cells. Anyone can find out that a substance has these properties as well as can anyone else, and so they are physical properties. Since these are the only properties needed for that particular body to be the body it is (= the only essential properties of that body), that body is a physical substance. Most physicalists hold that humans are the same as their bodies, but some other physicalists hold that humans are the same as their brains. The only difference between physicalism and mere property dualism is that, according to mere property dualism, humans do have some non-essential mental properties, and the events of their possessing these mental properties are not the same as and do not supervene on physical events, and may cause and be caused by physical events— for example, events in a person's brain may cause them to have sensations and thoughts, and their intentions may cause events in their brains.

The obvious objection to the view that humans are physical substances (in the sense which I have defined) is that if we ceased to have the capacity to be conscious, we would cease to exist. A dead person, no longer capable of becoming conscious, is not a person. So having this capacity is an essential property of humans. What constitutes me having that capacity is somewhat vague. Clearly I have that capacity if (whether awake or dreaming) I am actually having conscious events, or if I am in a dreamless sleep from which I will wake up as a result of normal bodily processes, or if I can be woken up by others, or if there is some process by which others can make me have a dream, or even if I am in a dreamless coma from which doctors with techniques not yet fully developed would one day be able to wake me up. But for persons in a deep, dreamless coma from which they cannot be woken up by any method which today's doctors are able to envisage, it is unclear whether we should say that they may still be alive (and so exist), or whether we should say that they are dead but could perhaps be brought back to life again by some physically possible (or other naturally possible) method. But it is clear enough that I do not have the capacity and so do not exist if I am not currently conscious and cannot be made conscious by any naturally possible method (that is, one possible, given the actual laws of nature, and so non-miraculous). Clinicians have various largely similar definitions of 'brain death', defining the state of a person's brain which they consider shows beyond reasonable doubt that that person is in that irreversible condition. (On this, see Chapter 7.) To have the capacity for consciousness is a mental property, because we have privileged access by experiencing it to whether we have this property—when a person is conscious, that person has this privileged access by experiencing being conscious. And since this mental property is an essential property of persons, and so of humans, we are not physical substances. Given my earlier definition of a substance as a mental substance iff it has at least one essential mental property, 'mental property' now being understood in the way defined in section D, it follows that all persons and so all humans are mental substances. So my argument has now brought me to the result that there are in the world not merely two kinds of properties and events, but two kinds of substances—physical substances and mental substances.

Persons are not the only mental substances. Fairly evidently the higher animals—that is, the mammals and possibly other vertebrates—are mental substances. For fairly evidently they are often conscious; and I shall spell out the evidence for this in Chapter 7. Since a higher animal who loses the capacity to be conscious is dead and so no longer exists, having that capacity is an essential property of such an animal; and so the higher animals are mental substances. But also fairly evidently no animal has moral beliefs; some animals behave altruistically, but they show no evidence of doing so because of a belief that they have a moral obligation to do so. Nor—in my view—do they have any capacity to do any simple logical reasoning, for to do that they would need to recognize valid deductive inferences. Because they do not have moral beliefs or the capacity for logical reasoning, no animals are persons—on my definition of a 'person'.

I now define a **pure mental substance** as a substance all of whose essential properties are pure mental properties, and an impure mental substance as one which has at least one essential physical property as well as at least one essential mental property. Humans, as I defined the term, belong to a biological species, and so have bodies and so physical properties. We have physical properties because our bodies have physical properties—we have properties of mass, size, and shape and the property of having heart, lung, etc. related to each other in certain ways, properties which are our properties because they belong to our bodies. If having these physical properties is essential for our existence, then we are impure mental substances; if they are not essential for our existence, then we are pure mental substances. If we, who are currently humans and have bodies, could—it is logically possible—continue to exist without our bodies and so without physical properties,[12] we are not essentially humans; we could cease to be humans, and yet continue to be persons. What I shall be arguing in the rest of the book is that we are essentially pure mental substances; and so, if we continued to exist without our bodies but continued to have moral beliefs and the capacity for logical reasoning, then we would continue to be persons.

3

Theories of Personal Identity

A. Different Kinds of Complex Theories of Personal Identity

Since the seventeenth century many philosophers have advocated 'complex' theories of personal identity. As I explained in Chapter 1, complex theories are theories which analyse the relation of personal identity, P_2 being the same person as P_1, in terms of relations between various other features of P_1 and P_2. Complex theories may be 'physical' theories, 'mental' (= 'psychological') theories, or mixed theories. Physical theories claim that the later George being the same person as the earlier George is analysable either totally or partly in terms of the later George having the same body and/or brain with similar physical properties as the earlier George, or body or brain or physical properties resulting from gradual changes in those of the earlier George. Mental theories claim that the later George being the same person as the earlier George is analysable either totally or partly in terms of the later George having many a-memories of what the earlier George did and experienced and perhaps also a similar character (= personality) to the earlier George, or a-memories (and perhaps character) resulting from gradual changes in those of the earlier George. While, as I wrote in Chapter 1, having the same personality (= character) as an earlier person is not the same as being that earlier person, a mental theory of personal identity, unlike a physical theory, may hold that being the same person is to a small degree constituted by having a similar personality. So a physical theory claims that a later person is the same person as an earlier person to whom he is connected by a causal chain of physical states of a body or brain, while a mental theory claims that a person is the same person as an earlier person to whom he is connected by a causal chain of mental states. Mixed theories combine elements of both physical and mental theories. By contrast, the simple theory of personal identity claims that a later George may be the same person as an earlier George, whether or not he has any of the same body or the same physical or mental properties (or body or properties continuous with those of the earlier person).

Different theories of each kind—physical, mental, or mixed—spell out the details of the kinds of continuity needed between earlier and later persons if they are to be the same person, such as whether identity depends on continuity of the whole body or just of the brain, and what constitutes 'gradual replacement' of properties or bodily parts. These theories are 'complex' because whether P_2 is the same person as P_1 depends on whether there is enough of various features—enough brain or enough accurate a-memories and aspects of character—and they often contain various exceptions and qualifications.

These rival theories are, I must emphasize, theories about what constitutes personal identity, P_2 at time t_2 being the same person as P_1 at an earlier time t_1. They are not as such theories about what causes a person to go on existing, and so what causes P_1 to be P_2. For a cause is not the same as its effect. An explosion is not the same event as the ignition of gas which causes it. So a mental theory need not deny that P_2 having many accurate a-memories of what P_1 did or experienced is caused by P_2 having the same brain as P_1, retaining many of the same connections between its neurons; but it denies that the existence of these connections is what constitutes P_2 being the same person as P_1. And the simple theory need not deny that brain (or bodily) events cause the continued existence of a person, and so cause the existence at a later time of a person who is the same as an earlier person. It holds merely that the continuing existence of the same person is a different event from these causes.

Also, these rival theories are not as such theories about what is good evidence that P_2 is the same person as P_1. However, in the case of all complex theories, the nature of the theory determines in a very obvious way what will constitute good evidence that its conditions for identity are satisfied. Thus on a theory that claims that the person called 'Susan' in July being the same person as some person called 'Susan' in June consists in the later Susan having the same brain as the earlier Susan, the best evidence that the later Susan is the same person as the earlier Susan would be provided by teams of observers who kept the earlier Susan under continuous observation and observed that her body became the body of the later Susan during the June–July period, when no one interfered with her brain. In the absence of such immensely strong evidence, as I noted in Chapter 1, these days we can have evidence almost as strong provided by fingerprints or DNA samples that the bodies and so the brains are the same, and so very strong evidence that the later person's brain is the same as that of the earlier person. But, in the absence of such strong evidence, P_2 having accurate a-memories of what P_1 did and experienced would be good evidence that they had the same brain, because P_2's ability to a-remember what P_1 did and experienced is best explained by P_2 having traces in her brain caused by P_1's actions and experiences, which in turn is best explained by the two brains being the same. Advocates of a simple theory will normally acknowledge that P_2 having the same brain as P_1 and being able to a-remember the actions and experiences of P_1 is good evidence that P_2 is the same person as P_1, and that the more that P_1's brain and a-memories are possessed by P_2, the stronger the evidence. But advocates of a simple theory need to explain why these things are evidence that the persons are the same, and I shall seek to do that in Chapter 7.

I understand by a 'strong version' of a complex theory of personal identity one which claims that whether a person P_1 at a time t_1 is the same person as a person P_2 at a later time t_2 depends *totally* on the degree to which they have the same body or brain and/or similar physical and mental properties (or continuous body or brain and/or physical and mental properties).

B. The Strong Body Theory of Personal Identity

The obvious strong physical theory is the body theory of personal identity, that a person P_2 at a time t_2 is the same person as P_1 at time t_1 iff P_2 has the same body as P_1. For a body B_2 at t_2 to be the same body as a body B_1 at t_1, it is not necessary that the two bodies be made of all, or even most, of the same atoms. We know that worn-out bodily cells are continually being replaced with new cells made of different atoms which we get from the food we eat, the liquid we drink, and the air we breathe, so that after seven years or so most of the atoms of a body have been replaced by different atoms. But as long as the replacement is gradual—a few cells are replaced one day, a few more the next day, and so on, and as long as the body has the same very general properties such as the same shape and most of the same parts (limbs, liver, kidneys, etc.) which are connected to each other in the same kind of way, or properties most of which change only fairly gradually—for example, someone grows taller or fatter fairly slowly— the body is said to be the 'same body'. This is compatible with one particular organ being replaced quickly, for example a heart being replaced by a heart taken from a dead person or animal. This view that a person is the same person as an earlier person iff they have the same body is often called 'animalism'; the criteria for the identity of persons and so humans over time are the same as the criteria for the identity of animals over time because humans are animals. So just as it might seem that a dog is the same dog iff he has the same body, so too for humans—according to animalism.

The body theory seems to give a clear and plausible answer to what makes two human persons the same under normal circumstances. But there may well be in future many abnormal circumstances where the replacement of bodily parts is not at all gradual, and so it begins to be unclear whether or not two bodies are the same. While a body may be said to be the same body when a kidney or heart is replaced, it is not clear whether we should call the body the same if many of its parts are replaced very quickly. And there is good reason to believe that every bodily part will soon prove replaceable. So what if all the bodily organs are all replaced with the exception of the brain? Surely the resulting body would not then be the same body as before. To replace all the parts apart from the brain in one operation could be achieved most easily simply by transplanting the brain into the skull of some other body from which its brain had been removed. Maybe this would only be possible if the brain being replaced was very similar in many aspects of its structure to the brain being transplanted, as would be the brain of an identical twin. Surgeons are only just learning to reconnect severed brain nerves. Even when they have learnt to do this, it will be a lot longer before they learn to connect enough nerves to reconnect a whole brain to a new body—since a brain has so many nerves connecting it to the rest of the body. But there seems no reason in principle why this should not be achieved. Yet if surgeons take your brain and put it into another body, would the resulting body now be your body, or would it still be the body of the person whose brain had been removed? It would surely now be your body, since you could now move its parts in the same way as you could previously move the parts of your earlier body, and you would now learn about the world through the eyes and ears of the new body. And so the resulting person would surely be you. For, as I argued in the previous chapter, we would not exist unless we had the capacity to be conscious—that is, to have sensations and thoughts, to form intentions, and to have beliefs and desires. Our brains are the immediate cause of our conscious states. Everything we learn through our sense organs we learn because of the messages they send to our brains, which in turn cause our beliefs; and everything we do intentionally with our bodies we do because we cause our brains to send messages to parts of those bodies—to our legs, arms, and so on. So if your brain was put into the empty skull from which someone else's brain had been removed and destroyed, the resulting person would surely be you; the other person would no longer exist. So, it would seem, you go where your brain goes.

C. The Strong Brain Theory of Personal Identity

Hence, among strong physical theories, the preferability of a brain theory of personal identity: that P_2 is the same person as P_1 iff P_2 has P_1's brain. The human brain consists of some 10^{12} neurons (nerve cells), forming different structures—the hypothalamus, thalamus, pituitary gland, hippocampus, and so on—themselves consisting of neurons and joined by bundles of neuron fibres. The lower part of the brain (the cerebellum) is responsible for organizing the non-voluntary operations of the body such as breathing and sleeping, and for executing our intentional movements (the ones we intend to make). The higher part of the brain (the cerebrum) is responsible for learning and memory, and it is events in the outer layer of brain cells of the cerebrum, the cerebral cortex, which—it is generally believed—give rise to conscious events (including our intentions). The cerebral cortex consists of two hemispheres, left and right. Neurons, unlike other cells, do not normally divide and form new cells after birth, nor apparently are outworn neurons normally replaced by new neurons; but stem cells—that is, cells not yet differentiated for a particular role in the body, to be found in some spaces between neurons—can divide to form new cells which can become neurons. But it seems to be the case that on the whole the neurons which give rise to your consciousness are not replaced every few years, and so they constitute a continuing base of you.

As mentioned in Chapter 1, surgeons can now remove parts of the brain, and humans seem able to survive when some of these are removed and even when the whole of a left or right hemisphere is removed. Patients suffering from otherwise incurable epilepsy due to a malfunctioning hemisphere sometimes have parts of that hemisphere removed, and on occasion even have the whole hemisphere removed in an operation called an 'anatomical hemispherectomy'; and the functions of that part or whole hemisphere are taken over by another part or by the other hemisphere. After that the patient often behaves fairly normally; in particular their a-memories and character remain the same, whichever hemisphere is removed.[1] When surgeons become able easily to repair damaged nerve connections, they should be able eventually to replace one hemisphere with a hemisphere taken from another person—for example, from an identical twin. And if they can do that for a whole hemisphere, why not for individual parts of that hemisphere or other parts of the brain, such as the hippocampus on which much of our ability to remember depends? There seems no reason in principle why this should not happen. And if surgeons were able to replace half of the organs of your brain with organs taken from your identical twin, the resulting person would have as much claim to be your identical twin as to be you—on a brain theory, since the resulting person would have as much of the brain of your identical twin as of the original you. In cases where P_2 came to have only somewhat more or somewhat less of P_1's brain, what might tip the balance is not the exact amount of P_1's brain that P_2 retains, but rather whether the operation left P_2 able to a-remember much of P_1's past life and to have a similar character to that of P_1. If P_2 recalled much of P_1's past life and had a character similar to his, we would probably say that P_2 was P_1, even if P_2 did not have quite as much as half of P_1's brain. That is, we would appeal to the mental criterion to settle the issue; and so we would be relying on a mixed physical and mental theory of personal identity.

D. Mental and Mixed Theories of Personal Identity

A strong version of a pure (that is, not mixed) mental theory claims that P_2 is the same person as P_1 iff P_2 has many a-memories of what P_1 did and experienced and perhaps also a similar character to P_1. In the years before the discovery of DNA, when there was no fingerprint evidence, and someone turned up claiming to be a long-lost person, the new arrival was cross-questioned to see if he or she a-remembered much of what happened to P_1. It was generally believed that the

Russian Tsar Nicholas II, his wife, and all their children were executed by the Bolsheviks in 1918; but a few years later a lady turned up claiming to be the youngest daughter, Princess Anastasia, who had avoided being executed. This 'claimant' seemed to be able to remember quite a lot of the experiences and actions of the original Anastasia, but far from all that she might have been expected to remember. In such cases, of course, there is a reasonable suspicion that the claimant is not being honest. But all memories fade in the course of time, and/ or are sometimes blotted out by traumatic events; and so someone's inability to remember much about their past life need not show that they are not being honest. So, if we assume that some person's reports of what they a-remember are honest reports, would that settle who that person was? They would need to be not just reports of the occurrence of events which the person did or experienced, but reports of apparent 'personal memories'; that is, of how it seemed to that person doing those actions and having those experiences 'from the inside'. If the claimant really (in this sense) a-remembered how it felt to her as she suffered seeing her parents and siblings being executed and much else in the life of Anastasia before 1918, most of the public content of which (what she saw and did) coincided with what could be discovered from other sources, would that constitute her being Anastasia?

In his *Essay Concerning Human Understanding* (published in 1690), the philosopher John Locke advocated a pure memory theory of personal identity that P_2 is the same person as P_1 iff P_2 has many a-memories of what P_1 did and experienced. Meaning by 'identity of consciousness', 'having the same a-memory', he wrote:

If Socrates and the present mayor of Queenborough agree [in identity of consciousness], they are the same person: if the same Socrates waking and sleeping does not partake of the same consciousness, Socrates waking and sleeping is not the same person. And to punish Socrates waking for what sleeping Socrates thought, and waking Socrates was never conscious of, would be no more right, than to punish one twin for what his brother twin did, whereof he knew nothing.[2]

Locke's theory needs tidying up in order to deal with the objection made by Thomas Reid in his *Essays on the Intellectual Powers of Man* (1785):

Suppose a brave officer to have been flogged when a boy at school for robbing an orchard, to have taken a standard from the enemy in his first campaign, and to have been made a general in advanced life; suppose also, which must be admitted to be possible, that, when he took the standard, he was conscious of his having been flogged at school, and that, when made a general, he was conscious of taking the standard, but had absolutely lost the consciousness of his flogging. These things being supposed, it follows, from Mr Locke's doctrine, that he who was flogged at school is the same person who took the standard, and that he who took the standard is the same person who was made a general. Whence it follows if there be any truth in logic, that the general is the same person with him who was flogged at school. But the general's consciousness does not reach so far back as his flogging; therefore according to Mr Locke's doctrine, he is not the same person who was flogged. Therefore the general is, and at the same time is not, the same person with him who was flogged at school.[3]

We can meet Reid's objection by reformulating Locke's theory as follows: P_2 at t_2 is the same person as P_1 at an earlier time t_1 iff *either* P_2 a-remembers much of what P_1 did and experienced, *or* he a-remembers much of what some person P^* at an intermediate time t^* did and experienced, when P^* a-remembers much of what P_1 did and experienced, *or* they are linked by some longer intermediate chain (that is, P_2 a-remembers much of what P^* did and experienced, and P^* a-remembers much of what P^{**} did and experienced, and so on until we reach a person who a-remembers much of what P_1 did and experienced). If P_1 and P_2 are linked by such a chain, they are, we may say, linked by mental continuity.

Some philosophers have claimed that for identity over time we need not merely mental continuity, but some degree of what they have called mental connectedness. P_2 is **mentally connected to P_1** to the extent to which she has a-memories of what P_1 did and experienced and somewhat the same character as P_1, not merely a-memories of what some person did or experienced who had a-memories of what P_1 did and experienced (or was connected to P_1 by a longer similar chain of a-memories and character). On this view, to use Reid's example, the general needs to remember a few of the schoolboy's experiences (and perhaps also have somewhat the same character as the schoolboy), if he is to be the same person. The American philosopher David Lewis discussed the biblical story that Methuselah lived for 969 years, and claimed that because Methuselah, or—more accurately—the person having mental continuity with the early Methuselah, would not have any a-memories of what the early Methuselah did and experienced, nor in any respect the same character 'after one and one-half centuries or so', we should consider it to be 'literally true' that the later person would be a different person from the early Methuselah.[4]

Clearly, the a-memories of the deeds and experiences of the previous person at each stage in the chain need not be completely accurate a-memories of what was done and experienced. But they do—on a mental theory—need to be fairly accurate memories of what was done and experienced, if the later person is to be the person who did and experienced those things. A person a-remembering that he did or experienced certain things involves the person having a belief that he did and experienced certain things. But it also involves the person believing that the former belief was formed by those actions or experiences, those actions or experiences initiating a causal chain of events which eventually caused him to recall them. Without a causal chain, it would be a mere coincidence that some memory belief was accurate; and if a person believed that there was no such causal chain, he wouldn't believe that his belief about the past was a 'memory' of that past. So we naturally suppose that a memory theory of personal identity can only be correct if our memories are formed via such a causal chain. Science has filled out for us the details of the normal nature of that causal chain, telling us that our experiences and actions make differences to our brains; that is, they leave 'traces' in our brains, which in turn cause our later a-memories of them. And, while some mental theories may regard brain continuity merely as evidence of mental continuity, most theories which regard a-memory as a criterion of personal identity insist on some brain continuity as a necessary condition of personal identity. And so we get a mixed physical and mental theory, which says that P_2 is the same person as P_1 iff there is some mental continuity (and perhaps connectedness) between them (for example, P_2 has many a-memories of what P_1 did and experienced or ones linked by a chain of a-memories) sustained by events in the same brain. And so on such a mixed theory the 'claimant' could only have been Anastasia if she had Anastasia's brain—although her a-memories constituted some (far from conclusive) evidence that she did have Anastasia's brain.

E. Objections to All Strong Complex Theories of Personal Identity

All theories which analyse personal identity solely in terms of degrees of physical or mental continuity or connectedness are open to one or two very serious closely connected objections. **The first objection, the arbitrariness objection**, which is an objection to all strong versions of a complex theory, is that on any such theory there will always be physically (or other naturally) possible borderline cases (and perhaps within a few decades practically possible borderline cases), where the answer to whether P_2 is the same person as P_1 looks totally arbitrary, lacking any justification. For all complex theories claim that whether P_2 at time t_2 is the same person as P_1 at time t_1 depends on whether there is enough of various features—enough body or brain or enough similarity between physical properties or enough a-memories. The theory might claim that iff at least 55 per cent of P_2's brain is derived from P_1's brain, P_2 would be P_1. But it would seem totally arbitrary to claim that replacement of 56 per cent of their brain changes the identity of a person, but replacement of 54 per cent does not. Perhaps '50 per cent' seems a less arbitrary figure, and so we should hold that if 50 per cent of P_2's brain is derived from P_1's brain, then P_2 is the same person as P_1, but if less than 50 per cent of P_2's brain is derived from P_1's brain, he is not P_1. But what if P_1 undergoes two operations—one replacing 49 per cent of P_1's brain and then a second operation replacing another 2 per cent? By the 50 per cent criterion, the person who existed after the first operation would still be P_1, and by the same criterion the mere replacement in a different operation of a further 2 per cent could not change the identity of the person. So everything would seem to depend on whether the replacement of brain matter was done in one operation or two. But how distant in time from each other do two operations have to be to constitute different operations? Any suggested time interval would seem totally arbitrary. And anyway, surely it is reasonable for some P_1 who knows that she is going to undergo a brain operation which would involve replacing 51 per cent of her previous brain matter to hope to survive the operation. It looks as if there is an important truth about whether P_1 will survive, which cannot be settled by an arbitrary philosophical definition of this kind. And the same applies whatever precise number, between perhaps 70 per cent and 30 per cent, we substitute for 50 per cent. And a similar objection can be made to every other strong complex theory, physical, mental, or mixed. If a mental theory specifies some particular number of a-memories covering some period of a particular duration a person needs to have in order to be the same person as the remembered person, any particular number which the theory specifies would be totally arbitrary. And note that in all such cases no further scientific investigation could possibly settle the issue of what is the correct percentage. For all that further scientific investigation could show is more details about the brains and a-memories of people who have survived operations or memory loss, and what the rival theories are concerned with is how to assess all the evidence anyone could ever get—whether to say that P_2 is P_1 when our evidence is that 55 per cent of P_2's brain is derived from P_1's brain, or whatever.

The **second objection, the more-than-one-candidate objection**, is closely connected to the first objection and applies to most but not all strong complex theories. This objection is that on most such theories it would be physically possible (and perhaps after a few decades practically possible) for there to be more than one subsequent person who would satisfy the criterion proposed in the theory for being the same person as the original person equally well. Just as there can be more than one later person who has quite a chunk of P_1's brain, so there could be more than one later person who has a-memories caused by P_1's past experiences, including a-memories caused via a causal chain which goes through a chunk of P_1's brain. I noted earlier that the removal of either the left or the right cerebral hemisphere seems to have little effect on memory or character, from which it follows that each hemisphere contains some of the brain traces (physically) necessary and—given that the hemisphere is functioning normally—sufficient for having many of the same memories and desires. Now suppose that the left hemisphere of some person Alexandra is put into the skull of another person Alex whose left hemisphere has been removed, and is connected to the rest of Alex's brain; and that Alexandra's right hemisphere is put into the skull of a different person Sandra whose right hemisphere has been removed and is connected to the rest of Sandra's brain. Then both the two resulting persons would have some of Alexandra's brain and should be expected to claim to remember quite a lot of Alexandra's actions and experiences. They could not, however, both be Alexandra. For if Alex is Alexandra, and Sandra is also Alexandra, then Alex would be the same person as Sandra. But subsequently to the operation, their bodies and brains are formed of different matter, and they live different lives with different experiences; and so they could not both be Alexandra. There remain three apparently possible outcomes (that is, outcomes apparently compatible with all that we could ever observe and experience). Either the person with Alexandra's left hemisphere is Alexandra, and the person with Alexandra's right hemisphere is not Alexandra; *or* the person with Alexandra's right hemisphere is Alexandra, while the person with Alexandra's left hemisphere is not Alexandra; or neither resulting person is Alexandra—for example, by both resulting persons being the same persons as the persons who previously had the parts of their brains which were not removed (in particular, their cerebellums)— that is, Alex and Sandra, who are different persons from Alexandra.

A version of any physical, mental, or mixed theory can always be crafted in such a way that only one later person could satisfy the criteria for being the same person as the earlier person. One way in which this can be done is by inserting a clause in the theory which states that if there are two candidates P_2 and P_2^* who satisfy equally well the criteria of that theory for being the original person P_1, then neither of them are that person; the person continues to exist only if there is a 'closest continuer'—to use the expression coined by Robert Nozick,[5] who advocated this view. But that is a very implausible requirement, for it would follow from it that in the scenario just described, Alex would be Alexandra iff Sandra didn't exist; and so whether Alex is Alexandra depends on whether some other person exists or not. Then if Alexandra knew in advance what would happen to her brain, she could ensure that she would survive by getting the nurse to ensure that one of the subsequent persons (it wouldn't matter which!) never recovered consciousness. But who a person is cannot depend on what happens to some brain which is never her brain. So, if we refuse to make such an implausible amendment, many complex theories have the consequence that there could often be two resulting persons who are (on all the obtainable evidence) equally good candidates for being the original person; and the resulting persons, like everyone else, will not know which of the previous persons they are.

I conclude that no strong complex theory can give a plausible answer to whether some later person is or is not the same person as some earlier person in abnormal cases, where the later person is on the border between satisfying and not satisfying the requirements of the theory; and many such theories will have the additional problem that there can be two equally plausible candidates for being a certain earlier person. So no strong complex theory can provide a universally applicable general answer to what constitutes being the same person.

F. Partial Identity Theories of Personal Identity

The only way for a strong complex theory to meet the objections that any precise version of such a theory would involve an arbitrary criterion (e.g. require the subsequent person to have 55 per cent of the brain matter of the original person) and often be satisfied by more than one candidate is by denying an assumption made in the previous discussion that it is always either true or false that some later person P_2 is identical with an earlier person P_1. Many of our concepts are such that for some object it is neither definitely true nor definitely false that the concept applies to them. When a surface is reddish-blue, it is neither definitely true that the surface is red nor definitely false that the surface is red. Harold Noonan[6] has suggested that what we should say when some later person is by some set of criteria on the border between being and not being the same person as an earlier person is that this is an example of what he calls 'semantic indecision'; that it is neither true nor false that that person is the same person as the earlier person. And so it would follow also, when there is more than one plausible candidate for being 'the same person' as some earlier person, that it is neither true nor false of each candidate that he is the 'same person' as the earlier person. Our concept of 'same person' is not designed to fit borderline cases, claims Noonan. After all, that is what we do say when we are dealing with the sameness over time of ordinary inanimate physical objects. If you replace only one of the four legs of a table, it is true that the resultant table is the same table as the earlier table; if you replace the top of the table and two of its legs, it is false that the resultant table is the same table as the earlier table. But in an intermediate case, when you replace three of the legs but keep the table top and one leg, our concept of 'same table' is not sharp enough to provide a clear answer to whether the resultant table is the same table as the earlier table; it is neither true nor false that the earlier table still exists.

But, despite the plausibility of this kind of answer to problems of the identity of inanimate physical objects, we can see its implausibility as an answer to the problem of personal identity, if we add a further detail to the earlier thought experiment. Suppose that Alexandra and two other unfortunate humans, Alex and Sandra, have been captured by a mad surgeon. The surgeon tells Alexandra that he is going to remove her cerebrum from her brain, divide it into the two hemi-spheres, put Alexandra's left hemisphere into Alex's skull from which her left hemisphere has been removed, and put Alexandra's right hemisphere into Sandra's skull from which her right hemisphere has been removed; the two hemispheres will then be connected to the other parts of the two brains of what were Alex and Sandra respectively. There will then at the end of the process, both the surgeon and Alexandra reasonably believe, be two conscious persons. The two resulting persons, they have reason to believe, will have equal degrees of physical and mental continuity (and connectedness) with the earlier Alexandra. The surgeon tells Alexandra that after the operation, he will kill one of these resulting persons; but he offers Alexandra the choice now of whether it is the person with her right hemisphere or the person with her left hemisphere who will be killed. Alexandra believes that the surgeon will do what she chooses, and she wishes to survive. How should she choose so as to have the best chance of surviving? On a 'semantic indecision' view, it won't matter which choice Alexandra makes, since whatever she chooses, it will be neither true nor false that she will survive. But surely there is a truth about whether or not Alexandra will survive. Or at least there may be a truth that Alexandra will survive or that Alexandra will not survive the operation if she makes a certain choice; and yet the 'semantic indecision' view has the consequence that whichever person is killed, that could not make any difference to the outcome of the operation. Yet it is surely (logically) possible, there is no contradiction in supposing, that, as with kidney or heart transplants, there is a truth about whether someone will survive an operation. It cannot be ruled out by some a priori philosophical theory that someone could survive an operation to remove some of their brain. When someone is about to undergo a brain operation of a more familiar kind, they normally hope to survive, and there seems to be nothing irrational in having that hope. How can this case be different, except in the respect that the doubt arises not from a doubt about whether the brain on which the operation is performed will ever again be the brain of a conscious person, but from a doubt about whether that brain will be the brain of the same person as the person whose it was before the operation?

The semantic indecision view holds that in almost all cases there is a truth about whether some future person will be me or not me; it is only in borderline cases that it is neither true nor false that a certain future person is the same person as a certain earlier person. But a semantic indecision view has to take a view about what are the boundaries of the neither-true-nor-false area. Thus, a semantic indecision version of a brain theory may hold that it is definitely true that P_2 is the same as P_1 iff P_2 has at least 55 per cent of P_1's brain, and definitely false that P_2 is the same as P_1 iff P_2 has no more than 45 per cent of P_1's brain, but it is neither true nor false that P_2 is P_1 iff P_2 has between 45 per cent and 55 per cent of P_1's brain. But this theory is now open to the arbitrariness objection—why take the neither-true-nor-false area as the area between 45 per cent and 55 per cent rather than the area between 40 per cent and 60 per cent? Any choice of the cut-off point as we take cases where P_2 is less and less continuous with P_1, where it becomes neither-true-nor-false that P_2 is the same as P_1, and any choice of the cut-off point as we take cases where P_2 becomes yet less and less continuous with P_1, where it ceases to be neither-true-nor-false that P_2 is the same as P_1 but to be definitely false that P_2 is the same as P_1, seems totally arbitrary. Hence it is natural for anyone sympathetic to the semantic indecision view to move to a more general view which I call **the 'partial identity' theory**: that a future person P_2 at a time t_2 is less and less identical to a person P_1 at a time t_1 insofar as there is less and less physical and mental continuity (and perhaps connectedness) between them. On this view it is only if t_2 is immediately after t_1 and there have been virtually no changes at all in body or brain or a-memory or character between those times that P_2 is really, fully, identical with P_1.

Different writers have used different expressions instead of 'partially identical' in order to state what is essentially a 'partial identity' theory. Robert Nozick wrote about later persons being 'continuers' (in physical and mental respects) of earlier persons; being the 'best continuer' and so being identical to the earlier person is just having more of what makes for continuity. David Lewis wrote of personal identity as 'a matter of degree' of a relation (of continuity and connectedness) which he calls the 'R-relation'; Derek Parfit wrote of later persons being (to different degrees) 'survivors' of the earlier person (to the extent to which they have physical and mental continuity and connectedness with them).[7] (Note that Parfit's sense of 'survive' is not the normal sense of 'continue to exist', since in Parfit's sense a person may have several different survivors at the same time.) The theory common to all these writers is that a future person being really 'identical' with a past person is just something like having a great degree (perhaps the maximum degree) of continuity and connectedness with that person, and a greater degree of continuity and connectedness with that person than with other persons. One consequence of a 'partial identity' theory is, as these writers admit, that one's concern for one's own future happiness is just concern for the happiness of some future person who has a large degree of continuity (and connectedness) with oneself, and so it would only be rational to have a similar concern (even if one of lesser degree) for anyone who has any degree of continuity (and connectedness) at all with oneself. This is not claiming that altruism (concern for others) is rational, but claiming that being selfish just is concern that people with much of one's own body, brain, a-memories, and character should flourish. Nozick, Lewis, Parfit, and most writers on personal identity who advocate a similar theory acknowledge that their theory seems initially implausible. But, they claim, that theory is the one to which reason leads.

There is, however, what I suggest is a conclusive objection to all 'partial identity' versions of strong complex theories. All such theories which allow the possibility that P_2 at a time t_2 may be partly identical to an earlier P_1 allow the possibility that there can be at the same time t_2 another person P_2^* who is also partly identical with P_1, although perhaps only to a lesser degree. Now consider another version of the earlier thought experiment where Alexandra knows that each of her two cerebral hemispheres will be transplanted into the brain of one of two future persons, Alex and Sandra, replacing both of their hemispheres. Suppose this time that Alexandra knows that something very good will happen to Alex—for example, that Alex will win a million dollars in a lottery, and that something very bad will happen to Sandra—for example, that she will be kidnapped and tortured. If the operation has the result that the resulting Alex is partly identical to Alexandra (or 'is a survivor' (in Parfit's sense) or 'continuer' of Alexandra (in Nozick's sense), or is R-related to Alexandra (in Lewis's sense)), then presumably Alexandra will have some good experience to which to look forward, but—since Alex is only partly identical to Alexandra—an experience which only a part of Alexandra will enjoy or which she will only partly enjoy or of which she will enjoy only a part. And if Sandra is partly identical (or whatever) to Alexandra, then presumably Alexandra will have some bad experience which she has reason to fear, but—since Sandra is only partly identical to Alexandra—something which only a part of Alexandra will find unpleasant or which she will find only partly unpleasant or of which she will find only a part unpleasant. So Alexandra will rightly expect to have one or more future experiences which in one of these ways will be mixed partly pleasant and partly unpleasant experiences.

Now it certainly makes sense to talk of an inanimate physical object being 'partly identical' to (and so 'surviving as' or whatever) each of two subsequent physical objects, in the sense that each of the subsequent objects includes different parts of the original object. Both the table formed from three of the legs of a previous table and the table formed from one leg and the top of the original table could rightly be said to be 'partly identical' with the earlier table. But although persons have parts, the parts don't have experiences; the person has the experiences. When I have a visual sensation and an auditory sensation at the same time, it is not the case that one part of me has the visual sensation and another part of me has the auditory sensation. Maybe one part of my brain causes me to have the visual sensation and another part of my brain causes me to have the auditory sensation, but what they cause is co-experienced. Whoever is aware of the one sensation is aware of the other sensation, and that 'whoever' is the person. So it makes no sense to suppose that 'part' of Alexandra can have some experience, which another part does not have; and so it makes no sense to suppose that the partial identity of

Alexandra with Alex and Sandra could consist in Alex already being a part of Alexandra and then subsequently having the pleasant experience, and Sandra already being a part of Alexandra and subsequently having the unpleasant experience.

But perhaps the partial identity of each of Alex and Sandra with Alexandra is not a matter of each being a part of Alexandra, but rather of Alexandra having an experience which she will only partly enjoy or of which she will enjoy only a part. Yet in the scenario which I have described, no one person has only partly enjoyable experiences, or experiences of which they enjoy only a part. Alex will have a fully enjoyable experience, not containing any unpleasant part; and Sandra will have a totally unpleasant experience, not containing any pleasant part. If the experiences of Alex and of Sandra were both in some sense also Alexandra's experiences, then whoever has one experience should be to some degree aware of having the other experience. For if someone is not to any degree aware of some experience, that experience is not in any sense their experience. But in the suggested scenario Alex and Sandra are different persons from each other and have different lives, unaware of each other's thoughts and feelings. I conclude that it does not make any sense to talk of a person being 'partly identical' with an earlier person; and so that the theories of Nozick, Lewis, and Parfit claiming that the identity of a person with an earlier person is simply the maximum degree of a relation of which there are degrees are mistaken.

Derek Parfit imagined a spectrum of cases where a different proportion of the neurons of each brain is replaced by new neurons. In one brain 1 per cent of the neurons are replaced, in the next brain 2 per cent are replaced, and so on until we get to a brain where 99 per cent of the neurons are replaced. Parfit points out that the simple theory is committed to the claim that there is a precise point along this spectrum where the tiniest extra replacement of one neuron causes the existence of a different person. He writes that this claim 'is hard to believe'.[8] But at least it is comprehensible; it is easy to understand the claim that there is such a precise point. The trouble with the supposition of 'partial identity' is that it is not comprehensible. I suppose that why Parfit finds the claim that there is such a precise point 'hard to believe' is because he supposes that a small difference in a cause can only make a small difference in its effect. But much recent science has shown that sometimes a small difference in a cause can make a very large difference in its effect. For example, chaos theory has taught us that a butterfly flapping its wing in one part of the world can cause a hurricane in another part of the world a few days later. And the brain is a system in which very small changes can sometimes produce very big effects very quickly. A very small change in the amount of neurotransmitter chemical released at a synapse (the narrow space between adjacent neurons) or in the exact width of the synapse determines whether electric potential is transmitted from one neuron to the next neurone, so as to cause the latter neuron to 'fire'; and one neuron firing can cause many other neurons to fire. So there is no good reason to suppose that a very small change in the number of neurons replaced in Parfit's spectrum cannot make all the difference to who the resulting person is.

G. Weak Complex Theories of Personal Identity

The strong complex theories which I considered earlier and which—I have been arguing—collapse into nonsensical 'partial identity' theories all claim that personal identity consists totally in, and is fully analysable in terms of, having a certain degree of continuity or connectedness. In other words, these theories all give both necessary and sufficient conditions for a person P_2 at time t_2 to be the same person as a person P_1 at time t_1. The conditions are necessary because P_2 would not be the same person as P_1 unless these conditions were satisfied; and the conditions are sufficient because P_2 would inevitably be the same person as P_1, if these conditions are satisfied. But there can be complex theories, of a kind which I shall call **'weak theories' of personal identity**, which state that personal identity depends only in a limited way on having a certain degree of continuity or connectedness of body or brain, or of physical or mental properties. Such a theory states only necessary *or* only sufficient conditions for P_2 to be the same as P_1. Thus there might be a theory, which I'll call the N-theory, that claims that it is necessary if P_2 is to be the same as P_1 that there is a certain degree of continuity of a-memory between P_1 and P_2, but allows that—even so—P_2 might still not be the same person as P_1. The N-theory says that the 'extra' in addition to this continuity, which would make P_2 the same person as P_1, cannot be analysed. And there might be a theory, which I'll call the S-theory, that claims that it is sufficient if P_2 is to be the same as P_1 that there is a certain degree of continuity of a-memory between P_1 and P_2, but allows that—even so—P_2 might still be the same as P_1, even if P_2 did not satisfy that requirement. It claims that the 'extra' which would make P_2 the same person as P_1 if the continuity requirement were not satisfied cannot be analysed. And there could be weak versions of all other body, brain, memory, and character theories, which specify only necessary or only sufficient conditions for personal identity.

But theories of these kinds are still open to the arbitrariness objection which applies to all strong theories, and leads to partial identity versions of those theories. If, for example, the N-theory specifies a precise degree of continuity of memory (or whatever) which is necessary if P_2 is to be the same person as P_1, perhaps the requirement that P_2 needs to have accurate a-memories of twenty of P_1's experiences, the choice of that precise number would be totally arbitrary. Surely P_1 might well survive even if he had only nineteen such accurate memories. So the theory must allow that there can always be borderline cases for satisfying any such requirement, which would force the theory into a 'partial identity' version. The N-theory would be forced to say that if P_2 did not have quite enough of the required degree of a-memory continuity with P_1, P_2 would be a borderline case for having enough continuity for the 'extra' to make that person P_1, and so could not be fully identical with P_1 but could be 'partly identical' with P_1, so long as P_2 had the 'extra'. But, once one allows borderline cases, it is arbitrary what counts as 'not quite enough' as opposed to 'not enough' continuity—that is, it is arbitrary where one draws the borders of 'the area of borderline cases'; and that forces us to say simply that the more continuity P_2 has with P_1, below the minimum degree needed to satisfy the N-theory's requirements, the greater would be the partial identity of P_2 with P_1, so long as P_2 had the 'extra'. And the S-theory would be forced to say that some person who did not have quite enough of the required degree of a-memory continuity with P_1 could still be a borderline case for having enough continuity to make that person P_1, and so could be 'partly identical' with P_1. And since it is arbitrary what counts as 'not quite enough' continuity, that forces us to say simply that the more continuity P_2 has with P_1, below the minimum degree needed to satisfy the S-theory's requirements, the greater the partial identity of P_2 with P_1. Since—given my earlier arguments—persons cannot be 'partly identical' to other persons, the N-theory and the S-theory both have an impossible consequence and so must fail.

Any other theory which claims that some continuity or connectedness of body or brain or of physical or mental properties is either sufficient or necessary for personal identity must fail for the same reasons. Although such a theory might seem to have no problems in cases where the continuity (or whatever) condition is definitely satisfied or definitely not satisfied, it must avoid the implausible arbitrariness involved in laying down any very precise boundary between satisfaction and non-satisfaction of the condition. It must therefore allow that there could be borderline cases for satisfying its condition, with respect to which it would have to allow that it is neither true nor false that P_2 is identical to P_1. Yet it would be equally arbitrary to limit cases of 'semantic indecision' to those within some precisely defined 'border area'. So weak complex theories, physical, mental, and mixed, as well as the strong ones considered earlier, must allow that there could be many cases where one person is partly identical to some future person. And since it doesn't make any sense to talk of a later person being 'partly identical' to an earlier person, those theories also must fail.

H. The Simple Theory of Personal Identity

The failure of all such complex theories leaves us inevitably with the 'simple theory of personal identity': that there are no necessary or sufficient conditions for personal identity in terms of the degree of any feature of which there can be degrees. The obvious thing to say is that in all cases, physical and mental continuity (and perhaps also connectedness) with a previous person is evidence of identity with her, but does not constitute it. The more P_2 has of P_1's brain, and the more P_2 a-remembers what P_1 did and experienced, the more probable it is that P_2 is P_1; but being P_1 is something other than and beyond the evidence for it. And then there is nothing paradoxical about there being two candidates, Alex and Sandra, such that the evidence makes it just as probable that Alex is Alexandra as that Sandra is Alexandra—just as the evidence available to the police about who fired the shot that killed some victim might make it equally probable that each of two suspects was the murderer. It is always possible that although on the evidence available at some time about the amount of Alexandra's brain possessed by Alex and Sandra respectively and the extent of their a-memories of her, it is just as probable that Alex is Alexandra as that Sandra is, new evidence might turn up—for example, Sandra might suddenly a-remember many more of Alexandra's experiences—which would make it more probable that one of them was Alexandra than that the other one was. But it would always be possible that the new evidence is misleading, and no such evidence would establish which of them was Alexandra beyond possible doubt. And even if we had all the possible relevant evidence about how much of Alexandra's brain and how many of Alexandra's a-memories each of Alex and Sandra had, it could remain equally probable that Alex is Alexandra and that Sandra is Alexandra. We humans are not omniscient, and there are limits to what we can discover about the world, and this kind of case provides one such limit. In most cases, however, where there are no split brains or total amnesia, evidence about how much of an earlier person's brain and how many of their a-memories some later person had will give overwhelming support either to the theory that that later person is the same person as the original person, or to the theory that that later person is a different person from the original person. Such is the conclusion (to my mind) forced upon us by reflection on brain hemisphere transplant and memory continuity thought experiments, some of which are likely to become practically possible scientific procedures within a century or so.

While brain transplant thought experiments help us to see that personal identity is something quite different from the continuities of matter and mental life, they all concern cases of persons who have (both before and after the transplant) normally functioning bodies. When asking whether P_2 is the same person as P_1, I assumed that both P_1 and P_2 have normal human bodies, whether or not those bodies were the same body. However, as I argued earlier, the most that persons (in the sense defined in Chapter 2) need in order to exist is a properly functioning brain. For our conscious lives depend only on that. So if instead of being connected in the normal way to the rest of a human body, some person had their brain removed and connected to a machine which supplied it with blood and any other necessary chemical substances, excreted waste material, and delivered impulses to its neurons similar to those sent to the brain by sense organs, that person would still have some of the same kind of conscious life as persons with bodies have. They would be in a situation similar to that of 'locked-in' persons, who cannot move their limbs or any other bodily part, but are aware of what is happening around them. And even if these brain-only persons were deprived of neural impulses similar to those from sense organs, they should still be able to go on thinking. Such persons are often called 'brains in a vat'. The results of this chapter apply also to these persons; their identity with past or future persons is not constituted by any particular degree of continuity of brain matter or a-memory between the persons at different times; although the greater any such degree, the more probable it is that the later person is the same person as the earlier person.

However, there is the further issue of whether it would be logically possible for a person to continue to exist without a brain, as well as without any other bodily part. In the next chapter I shall discuss Descartes's philosophical argument designed to show that it is logically possible that we can exist without a body or brain; and so that the essential part of each of us, what makes each of us who we are, is a non-bodily part, a pure mental substance, a necessarily indivisible soul.

4

Descartes's Argument for the Soul

A. The Principle of the Identity of Composites

I reached the conclusion at the end of Chapter 3 that the only satisfactory theory of personal identity is the simple theory: that a person P_2 at one time being the same person as a person P_1 at an earlier time is not analysable in terms of their having some of the same body or brain or other bodily parts, or in some kind of continuity between their physical or mental properties. So if the two cerebral hemispheres were taken out of the brain of a person Alexandra's skull, and one of these was put in the skull of another person Alex from which the corresponding hemisphere had been removed, it would be logically possible that the resulting person is Alexandra and also logically possible that the resulting person is not Alexandra. So perhaps personal identity is totally unanalysable; either the resulting person is or she is not Alexandra, and that is all that can be said. That does not follow. If the resulting person is Alexandra, there must be some part of her which makes her Alexandra, which a resulting person who is not Alexandra would not have.

This is because of a principle which I call 'the principle of the identity of composites', that 'if a substance exists for a certain period of time and has certain substances as its parts, and these parts have the same essential and non-essential properties, then it is not possible if these parts exist in the same arrangement having the same essential and non-essential properties for that period of time that they could form a different substance from the one which they do form'.[1] Consider a certain car parked in a certain car park, which has existed for a certain time, made of certain components (wheels, engine, seats, etc.) arranged in a certain way, each of these components having had a certain past history. What the principle says is that there could not exist instead of that car a different car which has existed for the same period of time, made of the same fundamental components with the same (essential and non-essential) properties and past history, arranged in the same way. Any car so constructed would be the same car. This principle is logically necessary. It is not conceivable to suppose that there could be a different car which was exactly the same as the original car in all these ways; I suggest that we can all see that that is logically impossible; it makes no sense. There could only be a different car in the car park if something about it was different from the actual car; some (essential or non-essential) present property of it or some part of it must be different, or something in its past history or the history of its parts must be different. And what goes for cars, I suggest, goes for any composite substance; that is, any substance which has parts.

Now we humans are composite substances; we consist of brains (which themselves have many parts), heart, liver, etc. So we can apply the principle of the identity of composites to humans. It follows that at any time any human with a certain body (and so brain), made of certain component parts, arranged in the same way, each of the parts having a certain past history, and certain essential and non-essential mental and physical properties, would be the same person. There could not be at that time, instead of that human, a different human who had exactly the same body (and so brain) and exactly the same essential and non-essential physical and mental properties, made of the same component parts, arranged in the same way with the same past history. Now consider again the thought experiment described in the first paragraph. The resulting person is either Alexandra or some human who is not Alexandra. So if she is Alexandra, there must be something about her which distinguishes her from the possible human who is not Alexandra. And if she is not Alexandra, there must be something about her which distinguishes her from Alexandra. Yet each of these possible humans would have exactly the same body (and so brain) and exactly the same essential and non-essential physical and mental properties, made of the same component parts, arranged in the same way, each part having the same past history. Since the two possible humans (Alexandra and the person who is not Alexandra) would have all the same properties, they could only be different from each other if one has a part which the other lacks. And, since they have all the same bodily, that is physical, parts, they must differ in the respect that one of them has a certain pure mental part which the other lacks, which I will call their 'soul'. The resulting person is Alexandra iff she has Alexandra's soul, and she is not Alexandra iff she does not have Alexandra's soul. If she does not have Alexandra's soul, she must have instead a different soul which would distinguish her from any other person who had exactly the same body (and so brain) and exactly the same essential and non-essential physical and mental properties, made of the same component parts, arranged in the same way, each part having the same past history. More generally, there can only be two different logically possible outcomes of this kind of brain hemisphere transplant experiment—as, I have argued, there can be—if humans have indivisible souls and each human has a different soul, a different pure mental substance as a component part.

B. Descartes's Original Argument

So our soul is necessary for our identity; it is what makes us who we are. But is it the only thing which is necessary for our existence? Do we not also need our body? There is a well-known argument of René Descartes which claims that his soul is the only thing which is necessary for his existence. Since any of us could formulate the same argument about ourselves as Descartes does about himself, it would follow that our soul is the only thing which is necessary for our existence. Here is his argument, contained in his *Discourse on the Method* published in 1637:

Examining attentively that which I was, I saw that I could conceive that I had no body, and that there was no world nor place where I might be; but yet that I could not for all that conceive that I was not. On the contrary, I saw from the very fact that I thought of doubting the truth of other things, it very evidently and certainly followed that I was; on the other hand if I had only ceased from thinking, even if all the rest of what I had ever imagined had really existed, I should have no reason for thinking that I had existed. From that I knew that I was a substance the whole essence or nature of which is to think, and that for its existence there is no need of any place, nor does it depend on any material thing; so that this 'me', that is to say, the soul by which I am what I am, is entirely distinct from body, and is even more easy to know than is the latter; and even if body were not, the soul would not cease to be what it is.[2]

Many people have the reaction to arguments of this kind that it could not be possible to reach substantial conclusions about human nature from an argument which seems to be mainly about what 'we can conceive'. Thus Paul Snowdon writes that an argument of this kind 'does fall foul of the general precept that serious ontological conclusions should never be derived from theoretical requirements supposedly discerned in thought about personal identity'.[3] All the great discoveries about the nature of the physical world made by science in the last five hundred years have been the result of scientists doing experiments and making observations to test theories formulated with the aid of technical terms and difficult mathematics. So how could we reach such a big conclusion about human nature as Descartes purports to have reached by a short argument which relies on no results of experiments and uses no sophisticated mathematics? That is an understandable but mistaken reaction. Although there is much in this argument about what Descartes 'can conceive', it has a premise describing a datum of experience, a crucial logically contingent phenomenon—'I thought of doubting the truth of other things', of which all he needs is 'I thought', a premise true of Descartes when he was conscious and true of every other human who is conscious. All that the subsequent argument does is to draw out what is entailed by 'I thought', a premise which is apparently trivial but really astounding. What Descartes does is to draw attention to something totally different from the publicly observable events which have been the concern of almost all the successful science of the last five hundred years. This is our own conscious awareness, something about which we can be more certain than about anything else, and the argument merely asks us to face up to what that entails. All science involves deducing consequences from scientific theories; that is, it focuses on what is entailed by scientific theories. As I pointed out in Chapter 2, {a sentence (and so the proposition which it expresses) s_1 entails a sentence s_2 (and so the proposition which it expresses)} iff {(s_1 and not-s_2) is or entails a contradiction; that is, is not conceivable (= not logically possible)}. 'It is red' entails 'it is coloured' because 'it is red and not coloured' entails the contradiction 'it is red and not-red'. Let 'L' represent 'Newton's laws together with propositions about the positions of the Sun and the planets a year ago', and 'P' represent a prediction that Mars will be at a certain place Q tomorrow. Then L entails P, iff (L and not-P) entail a contradiction; that is, 'is not conceivable'. So all science and indeed all deductive reasoning about anything at all assumes intuitions about what is and what is not conceivable, what is and what is not logically possible. So 'theoretical requirements supposedly discerned in thought' are vital for all science; and there is nothing in the least unscientific about deriving 'serious ontological conclusions' from the entailments of the astounding phenomenon of which all of us have infallible knowledge.

So I now proceed to examine Descartes's argument in detail. I begin by setting out the structure of this argument in my own words. Descartes's argument has in effect just the one obviously true logically contingent premise, and two premises about what he 'can conceive' and so about what is conceivable (= logically possible). He argues from that to the proposition, which I will call 'Descartes's lemma', that it is conceivable (= logically possible) that Descartes exists without a body; and he argues from that to his conclusion that he is a substance, 'entirely distinct from body', a soul. (A 'lemma' is a minor conclusion drawn from the premises, used as a step towards the final conclusion.) So this is the structure of Descartes's argument:

first premise: I am a substance which is thinking.

second premise: it is conceivable that 'I am thinking and I have no body'.

third premise: it is not conceivable that 'I am thinking and I do not exist'.

lemma: I am a substance which, it is conceivable, can exist without a body.

conclusion: I am a soul, a substance, the essence of which is to think.

Descartes assumes that he is a 'substance'. Although Descartes gives somewhat different definitions of 'substance' in different places in his writings, he would—I think—accept that all the things covered by my definition of a substance as 'a component of the world' are substances; and so in my sense Descartes is undoubtedly a substance. **Descartes's first premise** is the logically contingent premise that (at the time when he was considering this argument) 'I am thinking'. Descartes uses 'thinking' in a wide sense. He wrote elsewhere: 'By the word thought I understand all that of which we are conscious as operating in us. And that is why not only understanding, willing, imagining but also feeling, are here the same thing as thought'.[4] 'Thought' thus includes all conscious events. Hence, while considering the argument, Descartes knows this premise infallibly to be true. The eighteenth-century thinker Georg Lichtenberg famously objected that all that Descartes knows is that 'there is thinking going on', not that some person is doing the thinking. But that objection seems mistaken. 'Thinking' is a property, and there can only be an instance of some property if some substance has that property. And Descartes does not know merely that someone somewhere is thinking, he knows who it is that is doing the thinking—himself.

Descartes's second premise is that, while he is thinking, he can, compatibly with his logically contingent premise 'I am thinking', 'conceive that [I] have no body'. For maybe Descartes just dreams that he has a body. So he claims that he can conceive (= it is logically possible) that 'I am thinking and I have no body'. The premise that this is conceivable certainly seems immensely plausible to those who first hear it. For what is it to have a body? It is to have a chunk of matter through which one can make a difference to the physical world (for example, by opening a door by grasping it with one's hand and pulling), and through which one learns about the world (for example, by light impinging on one's eyes and sound waves impinging on one's ears, and one's nerves transmitting signals from eyes and ears to the brain). Some reports of 'near-death' experiences of patients undergoing an operation describe patients claiming to have experiences of floating above the operating table at the same time as the surgeons certify that those patients are 'brain-dead'. And while we may suspect that really the patients did not have those experiences at exactly the same time as they were brain-dead, or that surgeons may sometimes judge a patient to be 'brain-dead' while there is still some activity in the patient's brain, we can certainly understand what the reports claim, and fairly evidently they do not entail any contradiction. And what the reports claim is that at the time of the 'near-death' experiences, the patient had no contact with what was their body, and so they could not control any body or learn about the world through any body; and so their conceivable (though possibly false) claims were claims that they were having experiences at that time when they did not have a body. So—I suggest—Descartes was right in claiming that there is no contradiction entailed by 'I am thinking and I have no body', and so it is conceivable (= is logically possible) that I am thinking and I have no body. So his second premise is true.

Descartes's third premise is that he cannot conceive that 'I am thinking and I do not exist'. And it surely is obvious that that proposition entails a contradiction and so is inconceivable. 'I am thinking' obviously entails 'I exist'; and so 'I am thinking and I do not exist' entails 'I exist and I do not exist', which is a contradiction.

So he has proved what I am calling 'Descartes's lemma', that 'I am a substance which, it is conceivable, can exist without a body'. In his own words, 'for [my] existence there is no need of any place, nor does it depend on any material thing'. But, Descartes reasonably assumes, it is not conceivable that a substance could exist at a time without any of the actual parts it has at that time; and so if he were not to have a body and yet exist, then—Descartes claims—he must at that time have another part distinct from his body which would enable

Descartes to think. Descartes called such a non-bodily part his 'soul'. Since he could exist with only a soul, and the soul would exist as long as he is thinking, Descartes's conclusion is that 'I am a soul, a substance, the essence of which is to think'.

I suggest that the reasons which Descartes has given for proceeding from his three premises to his lemma are cogent and show conclusively that the lemma is true. But I now suggest that the step from the lemma to his final conclusion is not cogent. It fails for one minor reason and one major reason. I begin with the minor reason. The conclusion, which I have summarized as 'I am a soul, a substance, the essence of which is to think', in Descartes's own words the claim that he is a substance 'the whole essence or nature of which is to think', seems to mean that he exists when and only when he is thinking. But while 'I think' entails 'I exist', it does not follow that I cannot exist while I am not thinking, for example while I am in a dreamless sleep. And the only grounds which Descartes provides in the passage quoted for his claim that he is 'a substance, the whole essence or nature of which is to think' is that the fact that he is 'thinking' is his only reason for supposing that he exists. Yet that does not rule out the possibility that, unknown to him, he continues to exist while he is not thinking. Elsewhere in his writing, however, Descartes seems to suppose that we are conscious and so 'thinking' all the time; really there is no dreamless sleep, it is simply that we do not remember all our dreams.[5] But he does not need such a dubious hypothesis for his main argument. Descartes is, however, right to assume, for the reason I gave in Chapter 2 that the property of the capacity for being conscious is an essential property of all persons, that if he ceased to have the capacity for consciousness, he would cease to exist. So, while he does not argue that point in the quoted passage, I suggest that in proving that he is a substance who does not need a body and so any physical properties in order to exist, so long as he has the capacity for thought, he has proved that he is a substance, whose only essential property is the capacity for thought. Hence I suggest we attribute to him the **amended conclusion that 'I am a substance, a soul, whose only essential property is the capacity for thought'.**

Descartes's major error in arguing from his lemma to his conclusion is this. The lemma claims, 'I am a substance which, it is conceivable, can exist without a body'. But all that that shows is that it is logically possible that he could 'now' (that is, at the time when he is formulating his argument) be existing without a body and so with only a different part—a soul. It does not follow that he actually has a soul now. It shows only that if he has a soul, he exists; it does not show that he could not exist without a soul; that is, it shows that having a soul is sufficient for his existence, not that it is necessary for his existence. For maybe what is necessary *and* sufficient for Descartes to exist, what his whole essence consists in, is 'to have either a body or a soul (or both)'. If he had come into existence without a body (as his argument shows to be logically possible), then in that case he would have had a soul which would then have done the thinking. But in fact he has a body, and so maybe his body does the thinking, and he does not have a soul. So the conclusion that Descartes is essentially a soul does not follow.

However, I have already argued from 'the principle of the identity of composites' that having a soul is necessary for the existence of a person. So from that, together with Descartes's sound conclusion that having a soul is sufficient for his existence, it follows that having a soul is both necessary and sufficient for Descartes's existence. Taken together, these results show that having a soul is the only thing necessary for Descartes's existence. Further, I now proceed to show that it is quite easy to strengthen Descartes's argument so that (even without the argument from the principle of the identity of composites) it entails the conclusion that having a soul is both necessary and sufficient for his existence.

C. My Amended Version of Descartes's Argument

In order to show this, Descartes needs a stronger form of his second premise that it is conceivable, that is logically possible, that 'I am thinking and I have no body'. He needs instead **the amended second premise that it is conceivable that 'While I am thinking, my body is**

suddenly destroyed' (that is, in the middle of a period while I am now thinking my body is suddenly destroyed). I suggest that this stronger principle is also correct. If it is conceivable that while I am now thinking, I have no body, it is surely conceivable that while I am now thinking, I suddenly cease to have any control over my body or to be influenced by anything that happens in it; and in that case I would have ceased to 'have' a body; the body would be un-owned by me. Many of the reports of 'near-death' experiences of patients were of experiences of leaving their bodies; and while again we may reasonably doubt whether the patients really left their bodies, we can understand what their claims to have left their bodies mean—that they were at one time embodied and then left their bodies and observed them from a distance. Fairly evidently these claims do not entail contradictions. So if it is conceivable that I 'observe' while I cease to have a body, it is conceivable that I remain conscious when my body has been destroyed; 'while I am thinking, my body is suddenly destroyed' is conceivable. Then there follows from the amended second premise and the third premise what I will call the **amended lemma that 'I am a substance which, it is conceivable, can continue to exist while my body is suddenly destroyed'.**

I now add what I will call **the fourth premise, that it is inconceivable that any substance can lose all its parts simultaneously and yet continue to exist**—which is a more precise form of the principle which I suggested earlier that Descartes reasonably assumes. A table may continue to exist if it loses a leg, but not if it loses all its legs and the table top at the same time. And organisms can continue to exist if over time they lose all their parts, so long as those parts are gradually replaced, each part being replaced over a period of time while other parts continue to exist. A tree can continue to exist if each cell is replaced by a similar cell at different times. But what is inconceivable is that every single part of the tree should be suddenly destroyed and yet that tree should continue to exist. It follows from this fourth premise and the amended lemma that it is conceivable that now while Descartes has a body that body is suddenly destroyed and yet he continues to exist, that he must actually have now also another part which is not destroyed and which is doing the thinking, and which he and I are calling his 'soul'. For if he didn't already have that other part when his body is destroyed, he could not continue to exist. And since at any time while he is thinking and has a body, it is conceivable that he should lose his body and yet continue to exist, it follows that at every time while he is thinking, he has a soul. For if at some time he did not have a soul, it would be logically impossible that at that time he should continue to exist when his body is suddenly destroyed. And since at every time when he has the capacity for thought, it is conceivable that he should actually be thinking, and that while he is thinking he should lose his body and yet continue to think, it follows that at every time while he has the capacity for thought, whether or not he has a body, he has a soul. The amended conclusion that 'I am a substance, whose only essential property is the capacity for thought' follows. By relying on a premise which claims that it is conceivable that he is conscious both now when he has a body and also if he loses his body, my amended version of Descartes's argument shows that having a soul is not merely sufficient for his existence but also necessary for that. Thereby it avoids the objection to the original argument, and is—I suggest—sound. The amended conclusion is true. Given that Descartes now has a body, he now consists of two parts—an essential part (his soul) and an inessential part (his body). So the structure of the amended argument is as follows:

first premise: I am a substance which is thinking.

amended second premise: it is conceivable that 'while I am thinking, my body is suddenly destroyed'.

third premise: it is not conceivable that 'I am thinking and I do not exist'.

amended lemma: I am a substance which, it is conceivable, can continue to exist while my body is suddenly destroyed.

fourth premise: it is inconceivable that any substance can lose all its parts simultaneously and yet continue to exist.

amended conclusion: I am a soul, a substance, whose only essential property is the capacity for thought.

But what would constitute Descartes's soul without a body having the capacity for thought (in his sense of having the capacity to be conscious), except Descartes actually thinking (that is, being conscious)? As we saw in Chapter 2, in order for some embodied person to have the capacity for consciousness when not actually thinking, there needs to be some process which will cause that person to become conscious after some time. This could be some normal bodily process which would cause the person to wake up after a certain time; or something which others could do to the person's body to make them wake up. So likewise in the case of bodiless persons—that is, souls not connected to a body—there would need to be some regular process as a result of which the person would become conscious again after a certain time, or some procedure (other than acting on the person's body) by which some other person could get them to wake up. Unless there were some such process, if a bodiless Descartes ceased to think and then later began to think again, there would be no reason to claim that he existed in the unconscious interval; very probably he would have ceased to exist, and then begun to exist again when he became conscious.

However, even if the only way in which a bodiless Descartes could have the capacity for thought is by actually thinking, it remains conceivable that at any moment in Descartes's embodied life, his body could be destroyed while he retains that capacity. Hence at every moment of his embodied life, he has a soul, the only essential property of which is its capacity for consciousness. It follows that he is a pure mental substance. And if the argument shows that about Descartes, it shows it about every person and so every human being. But, as I noted in Chapter 2, while every actual human being is a pure mental substance in the sense that that being could exist without a body, if he or she were deprived of their body, they would then cease to be a human being. This is because any human being belongs to a biological species, and so must have a body. But a human being who was deprived of their body but continued to be conscious would remain a pure mental substance, and—if they retained their moral beliefs and the capacity for reasoning—they would remain a person. Each actual human being is essentially a pure mental substance, consisting of two substances—a soul (the essential part) and a body (the inessential part).

The properties of a substance may belong to that substance because they belong to a part of that substance—a table may be flat because its top is flat, a person may be tattooed because their skin is tattooed. And since a person being tattooed makes the same difference to the world as that person's skin being tattooed, these events are the same event. Since a person's body has physical properties (e.g. weighs 70kg.) and parts (e.g. a heart) independently of its connection to a soul, a person has physical properties because their body has physical properties. Since it is logically possible that at any time any person could cease to have a body, and yet their mental properties could continue to belong to them, it follows that a person has mental properties because their soul has mental properties. (That is not to deny that it may be naturally necessary—that is, a consequence of some law of nature—for a person's soul to be connected to their brain, if they are to have some or any mental properties.) So a person having a physical property is the same event as that person's body having that physical property, and a person having a mental property is the same event as that person's soul having that mental property.

D. Aquinas's Theory of the Relation of Soul and Body

Many philosophers, and especially theologians, sympathetic to some kind of substance dualism consider the version of substance dualism advocated by the thirteenth-century philosopher-theologian **Thomas Aquinas** to be superior to that of Descartes. This is because it takes seriously the very close connection between our bodies and our souls, which Descartes's theory seems to ignore. I suggest that the difference between these two theories is almost entirely terminological, and that in the one real respect in which they differ Descartes is right and Aquinas is mistaken.

Descartes's use of the word translated as 'soul' is the same as that of the fourth-century BCE Greek philosopher **Plato**'s use of the word ψυχή, normally translated as 'soul'; for Plato, as for Descartes, a 'soul' is a substance separable from the body. Plato's immediate successor, **Aristotle**, however, understood ψυχή in a very different sense from Plato. He held that the soul was the 'form' of the body. Aristotle held that every substance consists of a form 'imposed on' (= 'instantiated in') matter. He meant by a 'form' the property constituted by the conjunction of the essential properties which make a substance the kind of substance that it is. So, Aristotle held, each substance of the same kind has the same form; and it is the 'matter' of which it is made which makes a substance of some kind the particular substance it is. Thus, to use the examples discussed in Chapter 2, the form of a house is being a building made of solid material, used by a small group of humans as the place where they meet and eat; the matter of a house is the bricks of which it is made. A particular house consists of the form of a house being 'imposed on' a particular chunk of matter. The form of a tree is having a trunk and roots of certain kinds, and growing in certain ways; the matter of a tree is the organic material of which it is made. A particular tree consists of the form of a tree being 'imposed on' the particular organic matter. Forms only exist insofar as they are 'imposed on' particular matter. So for Aristotle the human soul is those essential properties which someone needs to have in order to be human (a certain bodily shape, and certain ways of behaving and thinking). Hence, for Aristotle, the human soul is the same in all humans; what makes each human different from each other human is the matter of which they (that is, their bodies) are made.

From at least the second century CE most Christians believed that the souls of the dead exist immediately after death in Heaven or Hell or some other intermediate place, where they have some sort of conscious life, but are reunited with a body only later at the General Resurrection; and most Christian thinkers understood 'soul' in Plato's sense of a substance separable from the body. But Thomas Aquinas tried to produce a Christian version of Aristotle's theory that the soul is the 'form of the body'. Yet unlike the souls of inanimate substances and of animals, the human soul is itself, he held, a 'subsistent thing' and so in a sense a substance, something which is capable of existing (after death, for a period) without being united to a body; and, he also held, the soul of each human is a different subsistent thing from the soul of each other human. But, Aquinas held, although in an imprecise sense a subsisting thing is a 'substance', it is not a *complete* substance, and each of us is only a person and only a human being when we have a body as well as a soul.[6] It is not a complete substance because the nature of a soul is to be joined to its body. And since, he held, being a person is an essential property of each of us—to speak strictly—each of us does not exist until our soul is reunited with our body.[7] So Aquinas, like Descartes, held that there are two substances which compose a complete human being—body and soul; but, unlike Descartes, he held that neither of these substances are 'complete substances', and only together do they form a complete substance. I will call this view 'Thomist substance dualism'. It is often called 'hylemorphism', from 'hyle', the Greek for 'matter', and 'morphe', the Greek for 'form'.

Although Aquinas's theory is expressed in a terminology which purports to be Aristotelian, it seems evidently not to be such. As I have just written, for Aristotle a 'form' is what it is in virtue of the essential properties which a substance needs to have in order to belong to a certain kind, and so any two humans must have the same form; and 'forms' cannot exist in any place without being instantiated in matter— which for humans means in a body. Yet Aquinas held that each human soul is different from each other human soul, and that a soul can exist in Heaven or Hell or elsewhere without being instantiated in a body. In these two crucial respects Aquinas's theory of human nature is precisely the same as that of Descartes, expressed in Aristotelian terminology used in a very different sense from Aristotle.

But it seems to me that the only real philosophical difference between Aquinas's view about the nature of human beings and that of Descartes is that Aquinas claims that—to speak strictly—we do not exist when we have lost our bodies; only our souls exist. But Aquinas did think that at least the souls of the saints in Heaven (before they are joined again to their bodies) have conscious events of sophisticated kinds, for example that they 'have an unchangeable will for the good',[8] and hear the prayers of believers on earth and ask God to grant those prayers. But surely if the souls of the saints have this unchangeable will, the saints themselves have this unchangeable will. Aquinas is committed to the (to my mind) implausible view that my body cannot be destroyed while I am having some thought (as in the first premise of my amended version of Descartes's argument), since any such thought would cease to be mine when my soul loses contact with my body. Surely the thoughts and experiences of our souls are our experiences, whether or not our souls are joined to a body. In that I suggest Descartes was right, and Aquinas was mistaken; and that is what makes the version of substance dualism which I am advocating 'Cartesian substance dualism' as opposed to 'Thomist substance dualism'.

Aquinas denied Descartes's claim that souls are 'persons', on the ground that they are not 'complete substances'. There is a sense in which the nature of a soul is to be joined to its body: that, as I shall stress shortly, the main value of our existence consists in being able to interact with other people and with the physical world, and without a body—barring a miracle—we would not be able to do this. But 'substance' is a philosophers' technical term; and while, as I do, Descartes counts any component of the world as a substance, whether or not it is a 'complete substance' in Aquinas's sense, Aquinas uses 'substance' in a more restricted sense. So this difference between Aquinas and Descartes seems only a terminological one. For Aquinas would not deny that souls are components of the world in Descartes's sense, and Descartes might not deny that souls are not 'complete substances' in Aquinas's sense. Aquinas also held that human souls are not human beings. As far as I know, Descartes did not discuss whether human souls are human beings. But in any case on this point I think Aquinas was correct, because to be a human being one must have a body of a certain kind. The situation of a human who temporarily became bodiless but continued to exist and to have a conscious life characteristic of persons would be that they temporarily ceased to be human while remaining (in my and Descartes's sense) a person. If they were capable only of having sensations, they would not be persons, but they would still be pure mental substances.

However, Aquinas's claim that we are not 'complete substances' without a body seems to me to have the great merit of bringing out just how important for human life it is that we should have a body. The first reason for that of course is that bodies keep us alive; and by doing various things to our bodies, we can make our conscious lives better or worse in the short and long terms. We can enjoy good food or take some risk which leads to us hurting ourselves, and we can care for or ruin our health. But even if by some miracle we were kept alive without a body and could make our own conscious life better or worse by some non-bodily means, without a body we would not have a public presence. Having a body means that there is some place where other people can get hold of us, and we can get hold of them; and we can share the enjoyment of a common public world. We can interact with others by causing our bodies to do things which they can see, hear, and feel; and thereby we can make each other's conscious life better or worse. Nothing that I write in this book is meant to deny the crucial importance of our bodies for the value of our lives.

It is normal for contemporary philosophers to claim that Descartes's argument fails for a reason quite different from those which led to my amending the argument in the way I have discussed earlier in this chapter. Objectors normally acknowledge that the sentence 'I exist and I have no body' does not by itself entail a contradiction and so is logically possible. But what that sentence tells us depends on who utters it. Descartes is using it to reach a claim about the actual person referred to by 'I', himself, a person; and so what he is really claiming is that 'I exist and I have no body, given what "I" (as used by Descartes) refers to' is logically possible. If Descartes were a zombie, what he claims would be logically impossible. But the issue is whether it is logically possible, given that Descartes is what he is. The way in which most contemporary philosophers express this point is to say that while that sentence may be *de dicto* **possible** (that is, logically possible as a sentence taken by itself), the issue is whether it is *de re* **possible** (that is, logically possible for the actual thing, the *res*, picked out by

'I', to have the property referred to of existing without a body). But, contemporary philosophers normally claim, Descartes does not know to what substance he is referring by 'I', and so he is in no position to assess what is logically possible for that substance to be or do. And, they claim, each of us is in just the same position of ignorance about what we are referring to by 'I'. Maybe, says the objector, 'I' refers to the speaker's body or to some part of their body, and in that case it would not be logically possible for that speaker to exist without their body. Or maybe 'I' refers to some quite undiscoverable essence of the speaker, and so no one can know whether it is logically possible for the speaker to exist without their body. And of course, if this objection to Descartes's argument were correct, it would be an equally powerful objection against my own amended version of Descartes's argument. I will devote the next chapter to assessing this objection, and I shall conclude that each of us does know to what they are referring by 'I', and so we are in a position to assess what is logically possible for that substance to be or do. That will lead to certain further results about the capacities and nature of the soul.

5

We Know Who We Are

A. Informative and Uninformative Designators

The objection to Descartes's argument, to which I referred at the end of Chapter 4, was that what Descartes needs to claim in his second premise is that it is conceivable that 'I exist and I have no body, given what "I" refers to'. But, the objector claims, Descartes does not know to what he is referring by 'I', and nor does anyone else know to what they are referring by 'I'; we do not know what it is to be the person we are, and so we are in no position to assess what is logically possible for 'I' to be or do. Maybe, claims the objector, it is logically impossible for me to exist without my body, when I am the sort of being that I am. In order to examine this objection, I need to devote a few pages to discussing a crucial difference between two kinds of word (or longer expression) by which we refer to objects (substances, properties, events, or any other kind of object there may be). I must ask the reader to be patient with this diversion, the crucial relevance of which will become apparent only later. I shall call these kinds of words **'designators'** (or **'referring expressions'**); they include names or descriptions, such as 'David Cameron', 'the sun', 'the man standing in the corner', 'water', and 'sodium chloride', by which we refer to substances or kinds of substances; and predicates, by which we refer to (= denote, or designate, or pick out) properties, such as '2 metres long', 'square', 'feeling tired', and 'tasting of coffee'. I define a word as an **'informative designator'** iff it is such that if we know what the word means, necessarily we know what is the object (substance,

property, or whatever) to which it refers (its 'referent'), in the sense
that we know what it is for an object to be that object and so we know
what I shall call the 'essence' of that object. I define a word as an
'uninformative designator' iff it is such that even if we know what the
word means, we do not necessarily know the essence of the object to
which it is referring; that is, know what it is to be the object to which it
is referring.

We know what a word means (that is, the meaning common to its
use in different contexts) iff either we know its definition by other
words whose meaning we know, or we are able to recognize the
objects to which it applies. Some non-technical words are defined
by other words. A 'philatelist' is a 'person who knows about or collects
postage stamps'. Someone is 'influential' iff they 'make a difference
to the beliefs, desires, or behaviour of many people'. Someone is
'married' iff they 'have participated in a legal ceremony establishing
a union involving sexual intimacy and sharing possessions with
another person who is still living, a union intended to last for both
of their lives (and have not subsequently gone through a different
legal ceremony cancelling the first legal ceremony)'. The words which
occur in these definitions may themselves be defined by yet other
words. A 'postage stamp' is a 'label which may be affixed to a letter,
signifying that someone has paid for the letter to be sent to the
address written on it'. And many technical words used in science
are defined by other words. Being 'a molecule of H_2O' is being 'a
molecule consisting of two atoms of hydrogen and one atom of
oxygen'. A 'molecule' of some stuff (solid, liquid, or gas) is the
smallest unit of that stuff; a volume of water, for example, consists
of a large number of molecules of water. A molecule of each kind of
stuff consists of a particular number of atoms of one or more particular kinds (there are roughly a hundred kinds of atoms); and
an 'atom' is a particle or bundle of smaller particles. An atom of
hydrogen is 'an atom whose nucleus includes one and only one
proton'. An 'atom' is a particle or bundle of smaller particles. An
'atom of oxygen' is 'an atom whose nucleus (its central part) includes
eight and only eight protons'. But in the end, if we are to understand

what some defined word means, the words by which it is defined need to be understood in terms of words whose meaning we know in some other way than by knowing a definition of them, and that other way involves being able to recognize straight-off objects to which they apply. And the words used in the definition of 'H_2O', like the words used in definitions of 'philatelist', influential', and 'married', can be defined in this way.

Thus a 'proton' is a particle of mass 1.67×10^{-27} kilogrammes with a positive electric charge of 1.60×10^{-19} coulombs. We know what 'mass' means, because we know that 'mass' is roughly the same as 'weight', but differs from it in certain specific ways. We know what 'weight' means because we can distinguish between heavier objects which have greater 'weight' and lighter objects which have less 'weight'. We know what 'electric charge' means because we can feel small amounts of it, passing along wires to light up light bulbs. We learn what '1 kilogramme' means by being able to weigh substances on scales; and we learn what an electric charge of '1 coulomb' means by being able to use instruments which measure an electric charge of 1 coulomb. We know what numbers are by counting objects. We know what '10^{-27}' (that is, one tenth multiplied by itself twenty-seven times) means by learning what it means to reduce a quantity to one tenth of its value, and what it means to perform an operation twenty-seven times. As a result of this process we know what the words mean by which 'H_2O' is defined and so we know what 'H_2O' means. Many terms used in physics can be understood in this way in terms of smaller or larger amounts of quantities, some medium-sized amounts of which we can recognize straight-off.

So in order to talk about anything, we need a lot of words whose meaning we know in virtue of being able to recognize straight-off instances of them. And the obvious way in which we acquire such knowledge of the meanings of words is by 'acquaintance'; that is, by perceiving or experiencing paradigm instances of the correct application of those words. They are words or longer expressions designating some property or kind of substance like 'line', 'angle', 'red', 'heavier', 'longer', 'door', 'house', 'road', 'straight', 'side', 'shirt', 'walks', 'shoe', 'cat', 'dog', 'flower', 'taller', and numbers; and words important in human interaction such as 'label', 'ceremony', 'possession', 'face', 'mouth', 'arm', 'kind', 'friendly', 'talks', and 'kiss'. Or they are nouns referring to particular substances, such as 'Mount Everest', 'London', 'the Earth', 'the Eiffel Tower', and so on. Most of us can recognize red objects, lines on paper, the edges of a building, etc. straight-off. The normal way by which we come to acquire this ability to recognize things is simply by listening to other people talk or, more explicitly, by having at some time been shown instances of correct application of its designator, and being shown how these instances differ from non-instances. We are told that this, that, and the other paradigm objects (such as a ripe tomato or raspberry, a London bus, or a British post box) are 'red', and that various other objects (such as unripe tomatoes or raspberries) are not red. This process enables us to recognize new objects as 'red' or 'not red' in future. Likewise with the names of substances. We learn to recognize some substances straight-off—'that is the Eiffel Tower', 'this city is London', 'the Earth is this big physical object on which all humans live'. Then we can refer to other substances and properties by their relations to these substances and properties so defined. Thus a 'Londoner is a person who has lived much of his or her life in London and feels that that is where he or she naturally belongs'. (If a word is used in more than one sense—for example, 'London' can be used to refer not merely to the English city, but also to a Canadian city—the context of any sentence in which it is used will normally reveal in which sense the word is being used.)

Being able to recognize instances of the correct application of a designator straight-off, as I am understanding this, involves being able to recognize whether or not it applies to an object—under ideal conditions. Conditions are ideal when one's faculties are working properly, one is in the best possible position (that is, best possible location relative to the object) for recognizing the property (or whatever) referred to, and one is not subject to an illusion. Thus if someone had normal sight and then became totally blind, their inability now to recognize a face doesn't show that they do not know what the word 'face' means. If someone is too far away from two rods, they may not be able to recognize whether one rod is 'longer than' another rod, but that doesn't show that they do not know what the expression 'longer than' means. Further, the circumstances must not be such as to make a property look (feel, sound, or whatever) differently from the way it would look (feel, sound, or whatever) in paradigm circumstances (that is, the normal circumstances in which the meaning of the word is explained to new speakers), as for example when a trick arrangement of mirrors makes it look as if there is a door in front of us when there is not.

In the case of words whose meaning we know straight-off and so are able to recognize under ideal conditions whether or not they apply, we know—simply in virtue of knowing the meaning of the word—what it is for the object to which they apply to be that object; we know the logically necessary and sufficient conditions for something to be that object. For an object to be 'a door' just is for it to look, feel like, and behave like (e.g. open when pushed) paradigm instances of doors. For a person to be 'walking' just is for that person to be doing what we recognize as paradigm instances of persons 'walking' as doing when we observe them under ideal conditions (standing fairly close to that person in daylight, with eyes working properly, and not subject to some illusion). To be London just is to be the big city which we (that is, those of us who learn what 'London' means straight-off) recognize as 'London' under ideal conditions (walking around a big city which looks totally familiar, with eyes working properly, and not in another city which looks exactly like London). Hence these words whose meaning we know straight-off are all informative designators.

Most words which denote properties and so kinds of substance (such as 'proton') (as opposed to words which denote individual substances which have those properties), and which can be defined by other words whose meaning we know straight-off, are also informative designators; and so we can know to which object (that is, to which property), in the sense of knowing the essence of that object, they refer merely in virtue of knowing their meaning. Which property a designator denotes is a matter of whether the property satisfies the definition which gives the logically necessary and sufficient conditions for the application of the designator. For some such words it may take a long process of definition by words defined by other words to determine which is the property (for example, which is the kind of substance) to which it refers. But, as I have illustrated, 'proton' is an informative designator because it can be defined by words which are such that speakers can always recognize whether or not these words (e.g. 'weight', 'electrically charged', 'twenty-seven times') apply to some object, when they are in the best possible position relative to the object (which involves being equipped with the right instruments for detecting the object), their faculties are working properly, and the situation is not deceptive. And so being a proton just is being an object which satisfies the definition of a proton. In the case of both kinds of informative designators, whether we know their meaning by being able to recognize when they apply straight-off or via a definition, simply in virtue of knowing the meaning of the word, we know what it is for some object to be an instance of that word.[1]

By contrast, an 'uninformative designator' is a word (or longer expression) which is such that if we know what the word means (that is, the meaning which is common to its use in different contexts), that is not by itself enough to know to what it refers on a particular occasion of its use; that is, to know what it is for an object to be that object. Many 'definite descriptions'—that is, descriptions of an object which pick out that object by some property of that object, such as 'the tallest building in London'—are uninformative designators of that object. We may know the meaning of 'the tallest building in London' and so what property it designates, but when we pick out that building by it having that property, the expression 'the tallest building in London' functions as an uninformative designator of that building. It will enable us—together with information about the context (that is, how tall other buildings in London are)—to pick out that building. But it does not as such enable us to know what makes the building that building—that, I pointed out in Chapter 2, is a matter of its size and shape and what are the bricks of which it is made. And knowing the meaning of 'the car outside the window' and so what it is to have the property of being 'the car outside the window' does not put us in a position to know what makes that car the car it is. Likewise most 'indexicals' are uninformative designators. An indexical is a word like 'he', or 'you', 'that river', or 'now', the referent of which (that is, to what they are referring) depends on the context in which it is uttered; that is, who says it, when, and where. Someone knows what the expression 'you are a fool' means iff they know that it means that the person to whom the speaker is talking is a fool. And even if they do know the context and so know in a sense to whom the person who uttered this sentence was talking, they may not know what makes that person the person he or she is. Someone knows what 'that river' means iff they know that it refers to a river to which the speaker has just pointed or alluded, and even if they know who the speaker is, and to what he or she has just pointed or alluded, they may not know what makes the river that particular river—which is a matter of its location and where it is flowing from and to.

There are other uninformative designators, such that the essence of the object to which they are referring depends on some underlying fact which may be totally unknown to anyone. Obvious examples are words used to denote kinds of chemical substances in the early nineteenth century before the discovery of their molecular structure. For example, the word 'water' was used in the early nineteenth century as a designator of the actual transparent drinkable liquid prevalent in our rivers and seas, and of whatever has the same chemical essence as that liquid. People knew what the word 'water' meant—it meant being a transparent drinkable liquid prevalent in our rivers and seas or any substance which had the same chemical essence as that substance. But they did not know what the chemical essence of water was, and so they allowed that sometimes some transparent drinkable liquid to be found in some small river might not be water; and they could not be sure whether something (liquid or solid) which was not transparent or drinkable or in our rivers or seas was or was not water. That collection of observable properties— 'transparent drinkable liquid prevalent in our rivers and seas'—by which in practice they picked out something as 'water' is what philosophers have come to call the 'stereotype' of water. But, being unable to use the definition of water to discover for certain of some substance whether it was water (and so not knowing in a crucial sense the 'essence' of water) without having further factual information, they did not fully understand what it is to be water. During the nineteenth century it was discovered that almost all volumes of liquid having the 'stereotype' of water consist of molecules, each of which consists of two atoms of hydrogen and one atom of oxygen. And so chemists came to understand being formed of such molecules as constituting a set of necessary and sufficient conditions for something to be water, these conditions being defined in terms of informative designators whose application they could recognize straight-off (in the way described earlier).

It is not just 'water', as used before the nineteenth century, which is an uninformative designator for the reason that it picks out a kind of substance which is the kind of substance it is because of its underlying chemical essence. Something is 'salt' not because of its taste, but because it is NaCl, sodium chloride; and something is gold not because of its appearance and weight, but because its molecules consist of atoms whose nuclei have seventy-nine protons. Before the nineteenth century speakers picked out something as 'salt' in virtue of its characteristic appearance and taste, which therefore constituted the stereotype of salt; and they picked out something as 'gold' in virtue of its appearance and weight, which therefore constituted the stereotype of gold. So, more precisely, a **stereotype** of an object is a normally sufficient condition for something having the requisite underlying essence which makes that object that object, but not a necessary condition. Speakers recognized that something could be salt even though it did not taste salty, and something could be gold even though it was not yellow.

Although all such examples are examples of words used in past centuries as uninformative designators but which have now become informative designators because the words have now come to mean substances of particular chemical constitution ('water' now means 'H_2O'), there are now new uninformative designators in the literature of science. Many of the terms of astronomy or particle physics apply to objects solely in virtue of their causes or effects, while physicists remain ignorant of what being such an object consists in. For example, in recent years physicists have discovered a new kind of charge—'colour charge'. Quarks can have a 'red' charge, a 'blue' charge, or a 'green' charge; but 'red', 'blue', and 'green' are just names, not meant to suggest that quarks have a property in any way similar to visible colour. A quark is called 'blue' when it combines with other quarks in ways other than it would do if it was 'red' or 'green'; and so on generally. But physicists have no idea what it is like for a quark to be 'blue', and so what makes 'blue' quarks behave differently from other quarks. But one day they may discover an underlying essence of almost all blue quarks, and then discover that some particle could have this essence without manifesting it in the normal way in which 'blue' quarks behave.

Whether a word (or longer expression) is an informative designator depends on the rules for its current use in the language. A word is an informative designator of some object iff the rules for its application to the object are such that speakers who know what the word means (= know what is common to its meaning in different contexts) thereby know what is the essence of any object to which it applies (that is, a set of necessary and sufficient conditions for being that object). It is an uninformative designator iff the criteria for its application to an object are such that it needs either further generally available knowledge including knowledge about the context of utterance (as with many definite descriptions and indexicals), or future scientific or other empirical investigation (which might or might not be successful) to determine what are the necessary and sufficient conditions for being that object. An uninformative designator of the latter kind may become an informative designator if and when scientific or other empirical investigation makes what these conditions are public knowledge.

While all the names of chemical substances which I have been discussing are now informative designators for scientists (for whom 'water' now means 'H_2O'), they are often only uninformative designators for the wider public. While both scientists and the wider public understand, for example, 'gold' as meaning a kind of substance with a certain density which is normally yellow, and malleable, and whatever has the same essence as such objects, only the scientists know what that essence is. For the wider public 'gold' is an uninformative designator, and one of a particular kind. They understand that the word refers to any substance which has the same essence as the paradigm examples of substances which have the relevant density, colour, and malleability, that essence being whatever the scientists say it is. I shall call an uninformative designator an '[uninformative] deferential designator' of an object iff one of the properties which determine its meaning and so help to determine whether or not it applies to an object is that an expert of some kind judges that it applies. It is involved in the meaning of an uninformative deferential designator that speakers 'defer' to some expert to tell them to what it refers. So while the wider public means something different by 'gold' from what scientists mean, both groups refer to the same chemical substance by the designator 'gold' and know that they do.

Since most of the words by which we refer to properties and many of the words by which we refer to substances are informative designators, it is the case of most sentences that if we know what their constituent words mean, we know the essence of the objects to which they refer, and so if such a sentence is logically possible, it is logically possible that the objects referred to could have the properties referred to. This is because if we can refer to an object by an informative designator, we know a set of logically necessary and sufficient conditions for something being that object, and so are in a position to work out what is logically possible and what is logically impossible for that object. Thus, not merely does the sentence 'the earth is 4 billion years old' not entail a contradiction and so is logically possible, but it is logically possible that the object referred to by 'the earth' is 4 billion years old; and this is because 'the earth' and '4 billion years old' are informative designators, and so in knowing what these expressions mean we know to which substance 'the earth' is referring and to which property '4 billion years old' is referring. So we can work out whether among the properties which it is logically possible for that substance to have is the property designated by '4 billion years old'. But if a sentence contains an uninformative designator referring to, for example, some substance such as 'water' (as used in the early nineteenth century), then the sentence may entail no contradiction but what it asserts about water may not be logically possible for the actual substance picked out by 'water'. For example, even though 'water consists of molecules of nitrogen' does not entail a contradiction, it is not logically possible that the actual substance picked out by water consists of molecules of nitrogen.

The distinctions I have made in this section will allow us to analyse more precisely the nature of the objection to Descartes's argument. The objection—to remind the reader—is that what Descartes needs as his second premise is not just that 'I am thinking and I have no body' is logically possible (= is conceivable), but that 'I am thinking and I have no body' is logically possible, given what 'I' (as used by Descartes) refers to. Now if 'I' is an informative designator, it would follow from the logical possibility of 'I am thinking and I have no body' that 'I am thinking and I have no body' is logically possible, given what 'I' refers to. For if 'I' is an informative designator, that entails that in knowing its meaning one knows to what it refers. But if 'I', like most other indexicals, is an uninformative designator, one could know what it means without knowing to what it refers. So in effect, the objection is claiming that 'I' is an uninformative designator and we do not know to what it refers—it's like 'water' was before scientists discovered its chemical essence, and so Descartes's second premise is too weak to yield his conclusion about the actual person who is Descartes. And the same objection, if it were cogent, would hold against my amended version of Descartes's argument, the second premise of which is that it is logically possible (= conceivable) that 'while I am thinking, my body is suddenly destroyed'. What I shall claim, in response to this objection, is that 'I' is an informative designator for each speaker who uses that expression, but an uninformative designator for anyone who hears someone else use that expression; and that likewise one's own proper name, such as

'Richard Swinburne', is an informative designator for Richard Swinburne, but an uninformative designator for everyone else.

B. Informative Designators of Mental Properties

Having analysed the difference between 'informative' and 'uninformative' designators, I approach the issue of whether 'I' is an informative designator of a mental substance by the connected issue of whether the designators of mental properties are informative or uninformative. A major purpose of this approach is to argue that the words referring to each person's mental properties are informative for that person, but not for others; and so it is to be expected that the word referring to that person themselves, 'I', is informative for that person, even if not for others.

The words we use in describing physical substances and physical properties are words of a public language—English, French, Spanish, or whatever. Many of these words are informative designators, and so competent speakers of the language (or—in the case of technical terms—experts) know not merely what the words mean but what are the objects (substances, properties, or whatever) to which they refer (= what it would be like for sentences in which they occur to be true). But, as I argued in Chapter 2, persons have privileged access by experiencing them to their own mental events and so to the properties which occur in them. As David Chalmers put the point with respect to conscious experiences: 'In most areas of science, data are intersubjectively available: they are equally available to a wide range of observers. But in the case of consciousness, first-person data concerning subjective experiences are directly available only to the subject having those experiences. To others, these first-person data are only indirectly available, mediated by observation of the subject's behaviour or brain processes'.[2] And—I argued in Chapter 2—the same applies not only to conscious events, but also to other mental events of which the subject is not currently conscious but can become conscious. (I remind the reader that in discussing 'mental events', subsequently to Chapter 1, I am discussing only pure mental events—unless I state otherwise.) Whatever means others have for finding out about my mental events, I can also use. If they infer to my mental events—e.g. infer that I am in pain, or that I believe that New York is the capital of USA—from my behaviour (including what I say about those events) or from my brain events, I could also infer to my mental events in this way. But I can learn about my mental events also by experiencing them, and others cannot do this; and so each of us has privileged access to his or her mental events. For this reason the subject of a mental event is the only person who is ever in the best possible position to know the content of that event, the content in the sense of the property involved in the event that that person experiences. The only faculty involved in our awareness of our conscious events is just a faculty of awareness; that is, being conscious; and so inevitably our faculties are working properly when we have conscious events, and so when we bring our non-conscious mental events to consciousness. Hence—unless we are subject to an illusion—we can always recognize whether some predicate whose meaning we know applies to that property or not. Hence the condition for a word whose meaning we know being an informative designator is always satisfied with respect to all the words which we use to describe our own mental events. But, I now argue, only the person who has a conscious event (or other mental event) can use a word as an informative designator to refer to the property that is involved in it. This is most obvious in the case of sensations.

We learn to use the words which refer to sensations by experiencing the sensations, and we distinguish between different kinds of sensations by the physical events which normally cause them and/or by the physical events (or the desires to do certain actions) which they normally cause. We learn to describe some food as 'tasting of coffee' iff it tastes like the taste which coffee causes. We learn to describe a smell as a 'smell of burnt almonds' iff it smells like the smell which burnt almonds cause. We learn to describe an after-image as a 'red' after-image iff it has the same visual appearance as do the visual appearances of (and so caused by) certain paradigm public 'red' objects (British post boxes, ripe tomatoes, strawberries, etc.). We learn to describe a sensation as an itch iff it is the kind of sensation which causes us to scratch (or to desire to scratch) the place which seems to cause the sensation. For some kinds of sensations both their normal causes and their frequent effects are important for enabling us to pick out the sensation to which we are referring. We learn to describe a sensation as an 'acute pain' iff it is the sort of sensation which is caused in us by certain kinds of bodily events (such as being cut or burnt), and which causes aversive behaviour (causes us to try to stop the pain if we know how to do so, for example by withdrawing a hand from the cause of the cut or running away from the fire which is burning us, or strongly to desire to do so). But having learnt to refer to a particular kind of sensation by events which typically cause it or are caused by it, we are then in a position to refer to that sensation when it does not have these typical causes or effects.

The fact that most other people learn to use words denoting sensations in much the same way as we learn them, and seem to make the same distinctions between different sensations as we do (for example, distinguishing red sensations from green sensations, and the taste of coffee from the taste of chocolate), makes it probable that they mean by the words they use to describe their sensations what we mean by the same words. But it can sometimes be reasonable for each of us to doubt whether other people do mean by the word they use to describe some sensation the same as we do—because the publicly observable effects of the sensation (including how they describe the sensation) are *somewhat* different from the effects in ourselves. (If their reactions were *totally* different, they would be unlikely to use the same word to describe the sensation.) We learn what a 'red' sensation is by looking at red surfaces, and what a 'green' sensation is by looking at green surfaces. This gives to most of us the ability to distinguish between red and green objects. But it does not give this ability to everyone; red and green objects both look the same to some colour-blind people. So either red objects do not look to them the way they look to most of us and/or green objects do not look to them the way they look to most of us; and so either when they say 'it looks red' or when they say 'it looks green', they must mean that it has a sensory appearance different from the sensory appearance which we describe by these sentences. (Note that whether some public surface is 'red' is a public matter, a matter of whether it looks to most observers to be of the same colour as (to produce the same colour sensations as) certain paradigm objects. But whether a surface 'looks red' to a certain person—as I am using that expression—is a matter of the particular sensory quality which it has in that person's experience of it.) And in the case of many sensations and especially tastes, the different reactions which people often have to the same input from their sense organs support the hypothesis that the sensations caused thereby are sometimes different in different people. Some people like the taste of curry, others don't; eating it produces different desires—to eat more of it or not to eat more of it—in different people, desires about which they often tell us. There are two possible hypotheses to explain this; curry tastes the same to everyone but some people like and some people don't like this taste, or curry tastes differently to different people. It would seem highly arbitrary to suppose that the first explanation is correct—let alone to suppose that a similar explanation applies to all different reactions to tastes. So generally insofar as we have reason to suppose that experiencing certain physical events causes different sensations in others from what it does in ourselves, we have reason to suppose that the words they use to describe their own sensations have different meanings from the words which we use to describe our own sensations.

But the observable inputs to the sense organs of other people (what it is that they are looking at or tasting which causes them to have certain sensations), and their observable resulting behaviour which is caused by such sensations (how they distinguish between their sensations and react to them), do not provide the best public evidence we could ever have about the nature of the sensations which are caused by that input or cause that behaviour. This is because that input only causes the sensations by causing brain events which cause the sensations; and that behaviour is only caused by the sensations because the sensations cause brain events which cause that behaviour. Maybe one day we could obtain very strong inductive evidence from studies of human brains about which sensations some human was having when, and so about what she means by the designators which she uses to describe them. (Inductive evidence for some hypothesis is evidence which makes that hypothesis probable, although not certain.) The strongest such inductive evidence would be provided by evidence that a brain event of a certain type causes a sensation of a type in all humans to which they react in the same way and a different way from the way in which they react to any sensation which is caused by any other type of brain event. That evidence would make it very probable that every human means the same by the word which they use to describe the sensation so caused. Thus if there were evidence that a sensation which all humans describe as 'the taste of coffee' was caused in all humans by and only by a certain type of brain event, that would be strong evidence that—whether or not that brain event is caused by drinking coffee—all humans mean the same by 'the taste of coffee'. Whereas evidence that a brain event of a certain type causes a sensation of one type in some humans, which they recognize as different from the sensation of a different type caused in them by a brain event of a different type, when in other humans brain events of both types cause sensations between which they cannot discriminate, entails that one or other type of brain event causes a different sensation in the different groups. Thus suppose it was found that in some humans brain events of one kind caused by drinking coffee cause a sensation which they describe as 'the taste of coffee', and brain events of a different kind caused by eating chocolate cause in these same humans a sensation which they describe as 'the taste of chocolate'. And suppose that in other humans brain events of both kinds caused either by drinking coffee or eating chocolate cause tastes between which they cannot discriminate and which they describe as both 'the taste of coffee' or 'the taste of chocolate'. (So coffee and chocolate taste the same to all humans of the second group.) That would be strong evidence that one group means something different by either 'the taste of chocolate' or 'the taste of coffee' (or both) from what the other group means.

Yet human brains are so different from each other and so many brain events are involved in the causation of a particular mental event that it will be very difficult to determine precisely which brain events are involved in causing which sensations in different brains. And particular mental events cause so many brain events in different brains that similar difficulties arise with attempts to identify mental events by their effects—for example, with attempts to determine what people mean by 'an acute pain' from the brain events caused by their having a sensation which they call 'an acute pain'. But however successful we were in all such cases in discovering the same brain events invariably correlated with subjects' descriptions of their sensations, the evidence available to others than the subject would be only inductive evidence, evidence that by far the most probable hypothesis which explains the data of the correlations between subjects' brain events and their subsequent reports and behaviour is the hypothesis that everyone means the same by the words which they use to describe their sensations. At best we might regard it as highly probable that other people mean by 'taste of coffee', 'red sensation', 'the sound of middle C', and so on the same as we do. But only a particular person can be in the best possible position to know what he or she means by their descriptions of their sensations; and so only that person can refer to their own sensations by informative designators.

While people also have privileged access, as well as to their sensations, to their propositional events—to their thoughts, beliefs, intentions, and desires—the content of most of those propositional events (what they desire or think) is a public one, and so expressed in the public language; someone desires to 'eat that cake', thinks that he is 'eating that cake', and so on. So when subjects report the content of their thoughts, beliefs, etc., there is normally—after investigation to check that they are using the public words with their normal senses—little room for serious doubt[3] about what they are telling us about their propositional events. (And that is why I counted the desires to bring about physical events caused by different sensations as in effect 'public evidence' about the probable nature of the sensations.) But sensations are not propositional events (in the sense defined in Chapter 2), and the public evidence about what people mean by the words they use to describe their sensations will always make it only probable to different degrees what they mean.

It follows that expressions describing sensations function as informative designators of one's own sensations, but as uninformative designators of the sensations of others. Suppose that both John and Mary learn to use 'acute pain' as a designator of the kind of sensation which is normally caused in them by certain kinds of bodily events (such as being cut or burnt); and which normally causes aversive behaviour (for example, causes them to withdraw their hand from the cause of the cut or run away from the fire which is burning them, or to desire to do so). Then John means by his 'acute pain' a sensation of the kind which is caused *in him* by those bodily events and which causes *him* to show aversive behaviour. Whether or not on a particular occasion it has such causes and effects, he uses 'acute pain' to refer to the intrinsic character of any sensation of his which feels like that. But he will understand Mary's use of 'acute pain' to mean the sort of sensation to which Mary alone has privileged access, which is normally caused *in her* by those bodily events and which normally causes *her* to show aversive behaviour, whether or not on a particular occasion it has such causes and effects. So these bodily events and aversive behaviour form a 'stereotype' by which John can pick out a kind of sensation which Mary is having; he must regard her use of 'acute pain' as referring to a sensation of the kind that normally underlies the publicly observable phenomena but which may occur without those phenomena, in the way that 'water' refers to the publicly observable liquid which is the liquid, not in virtue of its publicly observable character but in virtue of the chemical essence which normally underlies that. So John understands Mary's use of 'acute pain' as an uninformative designator of a sensation.

But John's understanding of Mary's use of 'acute pain' is also 'deferential', because John understands Mary's use of that expression to mean whatever Mary means by whatever sensation of hers is picked out by the stereotype of certain bodily manifestations. The situation of John in understanding Mary's use of 'acute pain' to mean whatever she means by a sensation related to certain observable manifestations is thus like that of the unscientific public who understand the scientists' use of the word 'gold' to mean what the scientists mean by the essence of an object which normally has certain observable properties. But there is this crucial difference from the scientific case: that while the unscientific public can—if they so choose—learn to use 'gold' as an informative designator, John could never learn to understand Mary's use of 'acute pain' as an informative designator. This is because Mary alone can ever be in the best possible position to know whether that expression as used by her applies to some sensation of hers. And of course conversely—Mary can never learn to understand John's use of 'acute pain' as an informative designator.

In due course when we learn more about which of a person's brain events are normally caused by that person being burnt or cut, and normally cause that person to show aversive behaviour, we may come to ascribe pains to others on the basis of their brain events. Then when Mary claims that she is having an 'acute pain', John will understand her to mean by that that she is having a sensation of the kind normally caused in her by the brain events normally caused by being burnt or cut, and which normally causes the brain events which normally cause aversive behaviour. And insofar as the brain events which cause Mary to have the sensation which she describes as an 'acute pain' are similar to the brain events which cause John to have the sensation which he describes as an 'acute pain', John will reasonably believe that Mary means by an 'acute pain' much the same as he means by it. Such brain events would now constitute the stereotype by which each of them comes to their limited understanding of the sensation experienced by the other. But it will still be the case that John uses the expression 'acute pain' to describe his own sensation as an informative designator, but in understanding what Mary means when she says that she has an 'acute pain', he understands that expression as a deferential uninformative designator to mean by it the kind of sensation normally connected with certain brain events in Mary and which means whatever Mary means by it—although he normally has good reason to believe that sensation to be a sensation of the same kind as the one which he calls 'acute pain' when he feels it. And what goes for 'acute pain' goes of course for 'taste of chocolate', 'red sensation', and all other terms designating sensations.

C. Informative Designators of Mental Substances

Mental events are the events they are, not merely in virtue of the properties involved in them, but in virtue of the substances—that is, the persons who have these properties—involved in them. So finally, are the words by which we refer to persons informative or uninformative designators? I suggest that the understanding of the criteria for some word being an informative designator developed in this chapter enables us now at last to answer this crucial question. As when we analyse the meanings of words used to refer to mental properties, we need to distinguish the meanings of words used to refer to our own mental properties from the meanings of words used to refer to the mental properties of others, so too in analysing the meanings of words used to refer to persons, we need to distinguish the meanings of words used to refer to ourselves from the meanings of words used to refer to others. We refer to ourself by the word 'I'. I suggest that, as used by each person, 'I' is an informative designator of themself. We mean by it this person who is currently aware of some conscious experience which he or she can informatively designate. For we are always able in ideal circumstances—that is, when (1) our faculties are working properly, (2) we are in the best possible position for recognizing ourself, and (3) we are not subject to an illusion—to recognize when some substance is 'I' and when it is not. Each of us is in the best possible position for recognizing themself when they pick out themself as the subject of a current conscious event, as the person who is now having this pain or that thought. Then we are as close as anyone can be to the person being referred to. Under those circumstances the other conditions for 'I' being an informative designator are also satisfied. When I am referring to myself as the subject of a current conscious event, my faculties are in working order and I cannot possibly be subject to illusion. For an illusion would consist in the circumstances being such that I refer to someone as 'I' who is not myself, or I fail to recognize myself as 'I'. But I couldn't possibly have a pain and suppose that really it was someone else who was having the pain; nor could I suppose that really it is I who am having the pain which is in fact someone else's and not mine. Of course I could suppose that some pain which I am having was of just the same kind as a pain which someone else was having, but what I cannot be mistaken about is that I am having the former pain—because if I thought that I was not having a pain, I wouldn't be feeling anything. When each of us is referring to themself as the subject of a current conscious event, we are, in Shoemaker's phrase, 'immune to error through misidentification'.[4]

In a famous passage the enormously influential eighteenth-century Scottish philosopher David Hume wrote, 'When I enter most intimately into what I call *myself*, I always stumble on some perception or other [in my terminology, some conscious event], of heat or cold, light or shade, love or hatred, pain or pleasure. I never catch myself at any time without a perception'.[5] But no one is ever aware of any substance except by being aware of some property of that substance. We never observe a house without being aware of some property of the house, such as its colour, shape, or such like. So the mere fact that Hume is never aware of himself without being aware of some property of himself, such as his having some thought or feeling some pain, doesn't mean that he is not aware of himself. And what he is aware of is not merely that some conscious event is happening in someone, but that it is happening in himself; that is, in the person who is aware of it. He is aware of himself by being aware of some property of himself. Often he has simultaneously more than one conscious event, for example he has a pain, seems to hear a noise, and has a red image in his visual field at the same time; these are co-experienced in that they all occur to the same person. So Hume, like Descartes and all of us, is aware of himself as the person who is aware of having certain experiences.

Since (unlike most other indexicals) 'I' as used by me is an informative designator—for me, so too is 'Richard Swinburne'; and so is 'I'
and their own proper name—for each other person. So the situation is
similar to the situation with respect to description of our sensations.
Just as each of us is always in a better position than anyone else could
be with respect to describing their sensations, so too each of us is
always in a better position than anyone else ever could be for recognizing ourselves—and that is when we refer to ourselves as the subject
of conscious events of which we are currently aware. Others can only
pick us out as that human who has that particular body and/or brain
and/or makes certain memory claims (and perhaps has a certain
character) and refers to himself or herself as 'I' or by their own proper
name. Others mean by 'Richard Swinburne' the person whose body is
such-and-such a body, or whose brain is such-and-such a brain, and/
or who makes certain memory claims, has a certain character, and
refers to himself as 'Richard Swinburne' or 'I'. Since others do not
have the (not merely privileged but infallible) access to who the
person is to whom they are referring which I have, the use of 'Richard
Swinburne' or some indexical expression by others to refer to me
involves using it as an uninformative deferential designator. Yet
'Richard Swinburne' used with each of the two meanings picks out
the same person. To be 'I' just is to be the person who is aware of
himself as experiencing some conscious event, and not any person
who is not experiencing that conscious event.

Our infallible knowledge of ourself is an infallible knowledge of
ourself as existing at the moment at which we are aware of this. We do
not have infallible awareness of what we experienced at some past
time or even whether we existed at some past time, nor any infallible
awareness of what we will experience in future. Nevertheless, when
I believe that I experienced such-and-such at a certain past time, or
will experience such-and-such at a certain future time, I know infallibly who it is to whom I believe that such-and-such experiences
occurred or will occur. Others who believe that I experienced such-
and-such at a certain past time or will experience such-and-such at a
certain future time cannot know as well as I do what it would be like

for their beliefs to be true—because they do not have the infallible access which I have to the identity of the person about whom they have these beliefs.

It follows that Descartes did know to what he was referring by 'I' when he claimed that it was 'conceivable' (= logically possible) that 'while I am thinking, I have no body'. So, knowing a set of logically necessary and sufficient conditions for a person to be 'I' (consisting in being the person who is having certain experiences of which he is aware), he knew what it would be like for that proposition to be true, given to what 'I' refers; he was in a position to judge whether or not that proposition is conceivable. And the same goes for the similar proposition used in my reformed version of Descartes's argument, 'While I am thinking, my body is suddenly destroyed', which I claimed to be conceivable (= logically possible), given what 'I' refers to—a claim which I hope I made plausible by spelling out in Chapter 4 one way in which it could be true. So this (now) traditional objection to Descartes's argument that no one knows to what they are referring by 'I', which—if cogent—would apply also to my revised version of it, fails. And since each of us can use Descartes's argument to show the same thing about him or herself, all persons and so all human beings are pure mental substances; that is, substances having one and only one essential part, their soul. Each of us also has a body, but our body is a non-essential part of us. We are who we are independently of the body to which we are linked; and—if it were naturally possible for the stream of our consciousness to continue when our body ceases to function—it would be our soul and so we who continue to exist.

D. Each Human Soul Has Its Own Thisness

Since what makes us who we are is our soul, how does my soul differ from your soul? The simple theory of personal identity has the consequence that two different persons (for example, Alexandra and the person who was not Alexandra—see the beginning of Chapter 4) could have had (at each time in their lives) all the same physical matter of their bodies and the same physical and mental properties. So the two different souls which make the different persons the persons they are could have had (at each time) all the same mental properties. So it cannot be sufficient to make a soul the particular soul it is that it has had a certain past mental life—that is, a certain sequence of mental properties in the course of its existence. But although having had a certain past mental life would not be enough to make a particular soul the soul it is, could it be part of what makes a soul the soul it is—that is, could it be necessary for a soul to be the soul it is that it has had a certain past mental life? It cannot be necessary for the identity of any person who has lived a normal-length life that he or she had any of the later mental events of their life; it would still have been me who continued to live if I had been adopted by surrogate parents immediately after my birth and had had a totally different sequence of mental events thereafter. So if any mental events are necessary for the identity of some person, it must be the very earliest ones. But it does seem implausible to suppose that it wouldn't have been me who came out of my mother's womb at a certain time just because the foetus which turned into the baby who did emerge had as its earliest mental events qualitatively different aches and pains from the ones which I had. Having mental events of just those kinds cannot be necessary for that foetus to be the earliest stage of me. Hence the identity of a particular person is not constituted by having had any particular mental properties at past times. It follows that persons, and so their essential parts, their souls, have what philosophers call 'thisness' (= *haecceity*), which makes them and so their soul the particular person and so their soul the particular ones they are.

Let me explain what I mean by a substance having 'thisness'. It does look as if two different physical substances could exist at the same time, having all the same properties as each other. The American philosopher Max Black[6] asked the question, 'Isn't it logically possible that the universe should have contained nothing but two exactly similar spheres?' Each such sphere could have been of the same size and shape, been 'made of chemically pure iron', and, being situated two miles apart, each would have had the (relational) property of being situated at a distance of two miles from a sphere having all the same intrinsic properties as itself. And—I add—each could have had a qualitatively similar past. For example, the spheres could have been revolving around each other under the influence of each other's gravity for an infinite past time. So each would have had at each moment of time the past-related property of being spatiotemporally continuous with a sphere having the same intrinsic properties for infinite past time. The philosophical principle known as the '**principle of the identity of indiscernibles**' claims that there cannot be two substances which have all the same properties, intrinsic and relational, as each other.[7] Black's thought experiment powerfully suggests that, on the contrary, it is logically possible that there could be two substances existing at the same time which have all the same properties as each other, and so substances to which this principle of the identity of indiscernibles does not apply.[8] Each of the spheres must be different from each other—otherwise there would not be two of them—yet the difference does not consist in their having different properties. Now suppose that only one of the two spheres existed; since those spheres are different from each other, it follows that the world would be different if instead of the former sphere, the other sphere existed instead. So, if there could be two such spheres, then— whether or not the other exists—each of them must have its own thisness. It is natural to suggest that the difference between the two spheres must consist in their being made of different matter from each other—the chunk of iron which forms each of them is different from the chunk which forms the other. But in that case, since each chunk has the same properties, the chunk is what it is in virtue of its own thisness. Either each of the spheres or each of the chunks of which they are made must have its own thisness.

A substance has thisness iff the principle of the identity of indiscernibles does not apply to it; that is, iff it is logically possible that there could have existed a different substance which has all the same properties (relational as well as intrinsic, past-related as well as present) as the former substance. Thus an electron would have thisness if the world would have been different if instead of the actual electron there had always been a different electron which had all the same properties (e.g. mass, charge, and spatial relations to other fundamental particles) at all times as the former electron. Most physicists believe that fundamental particles do not have thisness; any electron which had exactly the same properties as the actual electron would be the actual electron. So these physicists must hold that the situation described in Black's thought experiment is not conceivable, given the actual nature of fundamental particles of our universe and so of the larger objects, such as iron balls, which they compose. But whether any actual fundamental particles have thisness is a disputed issue; and Black's thought experiment makes it plausible to suppose that it is logically possible that there could be such particles (and indeed perhaps in another world there are such particles). So it is not a fair objection to the view that humans have thisness that it introduces an otherwise unknown category into philosophy in order to avoid incoherence. As I noted, in the case of ordinary medium-sized physical substances, the thisness of a substance (if it has thisness) plausibly consists in the chunk of matter of which it is made having thisness. But if a soul has thisness, that cannot consist in it being made of different matter (since souls are not physical substances), nor can it consist of being made of some mental stuff, since any stuff is (it is logically possible) divisible; and (as I argued in Chapter 3), persons and therefore their souls are indivisible. So if the soul has thisness, it must be just a brute fact that it does have thisness. (And some kinds of fundamental particles do not seem to be 'made out of' any matter, and so—if they were to have thisness—it would be just a brute fact that they do have thisness.)

It follows that instead of me living the life I have lived, (it is logically possible that) there could have been a different person, different from me in virtue of having a different soul from my soul, who lived a life which was the same as my life in all qualitative respects. Indeed, there could have been any of an infinite number of different souls and so persons from myself who lived a life which was the same as mine in all detailed respects. If electrons had thisness, and the world were different in the respect that there had always been, instead of a certain electron in a certain place, a different electron with all the same properties, no one could have noticed any difference. But if the world were different in containing another person instead of me with all the same properties as me, someone—that other person—would notice the difference; everyone else would not notice any difference. That other person would know that he was alive, and that the world would have been different if someone else had lived his life instead of him living his life. And if I had lived his life, and he had lived my life, we would both notice the difference. It is a consequence of this that, although a human body behaving in a normal way (and perhaps in due course a human brain operating in a normal way) constitute the stereotype by which we can pick out another human being, there is no stereotype by which we can distinguish the particular human being whose body it is from any of the infinite number of logically possible humans that could have had that body instead of that particular human.

I conclude that each person, and so each human, is the person he or she is in virtue of having a soul with a particular thisness; that is, a soul which is just different from any other actual or possible soul but not different because it has a different property or properties from those of other souls. It is a brute fact, not further analysable, that some soul is the soul it is. Our pure mental properties belong to our soul, while our physical properties belong to our body; souls just are substances of a kind that have the capacity to have mental properties.

In the final two chapters I shall investigate two further issues about the soul. The first issue is what are the causal powers of the soul; and so whether our intentions and beliefs make any difference to what happens in our bodies. The second issue is whether there could be a scientific explanation of the existence and powers of the soul.

Appendix on 'Metaphysical Modality'

The question with which I have been concerned in this chapter is whether some proposition is logically possible, impossible, or necessary, given the actual substances, properties, and events referred to. In modern philosophical discussions logical modality (that is, logical possibility, impossibility, or necessity) given the actual reference of referring terms is often called 'metaphysical modality'. In Chapter 2 I defined a sentence as logically possible iff it is not a contradiction and does not entail a contradiction. Whether or not a sentence entails a contradiction depends only on the rules of the language and can be determined a priori; that is, determined by a competent speaker of the language, even if they do not know to what the referring expressions in the sentence are referring. In that sense clearly such sentences as 'water is not H_2O' (as uttered by an early nineteenth-century speaker) are logically possible. But in the late 1960s Saul Kripke (in *Naming and Necessity*, republished as a book by Blackwell, 1980) and Hilary Putnam (in 'The Meaning of "Meaning"' republished in his *Mind, Language, and Reality, Philosophical Papers*, vol. 2, Cambridge University Press, 1975) pointed out that the supposed states of affairs which such sentences as 'water is not H_2O' describe are just as absolutely impossible as 'Hesperus exists and does not exist at the same time'—since the actual nature of what is picked out by 'water' is that it is 'H_2O'. We can elucidate this distinction by defining a 'metaphysically impossible' sentence as one which is just as impossible as a contradiction is impossible, and defining a 'metaphysically necessary' sentence as one which is just as necessary as is the negation of a contradiction; and a 'metaphysically possible' sentence as one which is not metaphysically impossible. Then we can define a sentence as 'logically' possible/impossible/necessary as one which can be shown to be such a priori (that is, merely by knowledge of the rules of the meanings of the words) by its relation to contradictions—that it is logically possible because it does not entail a contradiction, logically impossible because it entails a contradiction, logically necessary because its negation entails a contradiction. And we can define a sentence as metaphysically possible/impossible/necessary a posteriori as one which can be shown to be such only a posteriori (that is, by knowledge of the rules of the language together with additional knowledge obtainable only a posteriori of which objects are the referents of the referring expressions). This distinction can be elucidated with the concept of 'a rigid designator'. A 'rigid designator' is a designator which always refers to the same object (substance, property, or event), whatever non-essential properties that object may gain or lose, or even always have. Proper names usually function as rigid designators. 'Richard Swinburne' refers to me whatever might happen to me, for example whatever my occupation or age; whereas 'The Professor of the Philosophy of Religion at Oxford' referred to me only when I held that position, and so is not a rigid designator. 'Green' is a rigid designator of a property; it always refers to the same colour property of a substance, whether or not that property has such non-essential properties as being 'Amanda's favourite colour'. But 'Amanda's favourite colour' does not normally function as a rigid designator of a particular colour property, since it refers to whatever colour is Amanda's favourite colour. It refers to the colour green iff green is Amanda's favourite colour; but if Amanda comes to prefer the colour red, 'Amanda's favourite colour' refers to the colour red. So all informative designators are rigid designators, but not all rigid designators are informative—for example, 'water' (as used in the early nineteenth century) is a rigid designator, but not informative. It then follows that a sentence is metaphysically possible/impossible/necessary iff it is logically possible/impossible/necessary when all its uninformative rigid designators are replaced by informative designators of the same object. Hence there are metaphysically impossible/necessary sentences (and so propositions which the sentences express) which are not logically impossible/necessary; and there are logically possible sentences (and so propositions which the sentences express) which are not metaphysically possible. So what I am claiming is that 'I am thinking and I have no body' and 'while I am thinking, my body is suddenly destroyed' are not merely logically possible, but also metaphysically possible—since 'I' and their own proper name are informative designators for the speaker, even if not for anyone else.

6

Souls and Bodies Interact

A. Brain Events Often Cause Pure Mental Events

I shall investigate in this chapter the causal properties of a human's soul, and their causal relations to that human's brain. I shall argue that not merely does the brain cause events in the soul, but the soul causes events in both soul and brain. I shall assume for the purposes of this discussion that to say that a brain causes some pure mental event is to say that a brain event causes that pure mental event, and to say that a person or their soul causes some event is to say that some pure mental event causes that event. So I shall be investigating the causal relations between pure mental events and other pure mental events, and between pure mental events and brain events. (Hereafter I shall again normally abbreviate 'pure mental event' to 'mental event', and ask the reader to assume that when I make some claim about 'mental events', I am making a claim about pure mental events, unless I state otherwise.) So do brain events cause mental events? Do mental events cause other mental events? And do mental events cause brain events? (By an event E causing an event F, I mean that E is a necessary part of the total cause of F; F wouldn't happen but for E.)

It is evident that brain events often do cause mental events. The input to our sense organs causes us to have sensations and beliefs about our surroundings; for example, when I look out of the window, I experience a visual image of a tree and I acquire a belief that there is a tree outside the window. Scientific developments of the past five hundred years have made it obvious that light rays, sound waves, or other causal influences from the public world impinging on our sense organs cause such beliefs and sensations indirectly by causing brain events which cause the beliefs and sensations. More recent science has made it evident that our continuing brain states and changes of brain states are a major direct cause of our having the desires about the world which we have—both the short-term desires for food, drink, sex, or sleep; and the long-term desires for fame or fortune. And it is plausible to suppose that brain events are also at least partly responsible for us having the occurrent thoughts and forming some of the intentions which we form at particular times.

B. Rational Belief

But, I shall now argue, it is very probable that mental events often cause other mental events, and that mental events often cause brain events. To show this, I need to investigate the nature of belief, and what makes a belief probable and so rational or justified.

I shall understand by someone having a belief that p that he or she believes that p is probable; that is, more probable than not. If I believe that the theory of evolution is true, then I believe that it is more probable than not that it is true. If I believe that there is a car outside the house, then I believe that it is more probable than not that there is a car outside the house. If I believe that p, then it seems to me that p (= it seems to me that p is probable). Our beliefs form what has been called a 'noetic structure'. All the time we are acquiring new beliefs and discarding or forgetting old beliefs. Our beliefs are of two kinds—basic beliefs and non-basic beliefs. Our basic beliefs are the beliefs which we just find ourselves having because they come to us naturally, seemingly produced by our awareness of how things are. Non-basic beliefs are ones which we hold because (consciously or subconsciously) we infer them from our basic beliefs. We believe our non-basic beliefs because we believe that they are probably true, given our basic beliefs (that is, the basic beliefs make the other beliefs probable).

Basic beliefs are of three main kinds. First, there are what I shall call **experiential beliefs** (= apparent experiences). The main such beliefs are perceptual beliefs (= apparent perceptions). These are beliefs about what we are currently perceiving; that is, seeing, hearing, or whatever. I believe that the telephone is ringing because I am aware of the noise of a ring which seems to me to come from the telephone. I believe that there is a tree outside the window because I seem to be seeing the tree. In both cases I have sensations—of noise and a pattern of colour in my visual field, but I do not infer the presence of the tree or the telephone ring from the sensation; rather, the belief comes jointly with the sensation. It just seems to me that there is a tree outside the window or that the telephone is ringing. I shall also include as experiential beliefs our beliefs about the mental events which we are having—for example, that I have a certain intention or pattern of colour in my visual field, or a certain intention in what I am doing. I shall also include those apparently obvious beliefs about 'truths of reason', such as that '2 + 2 = 4' or that '"all humans are mortal" and "Socrates is a human" together entail "Socrates is mortal"', which we seem to 'see' to be true when we reflect on them.

Secondly, there are **memory beliefs**, our apparent memories (a-memories) about what we did or experienced in the past. These are basic beliefs, because we do not infer them from something else but it just seems to us that we did so-and-so or experienced so-and-so. Thirdly, there are what I shall call **'testimonial beliefs'**. These are beliefs that someone is telling us something (their 'apparent testimonies'). If the words come out of your mouth 'it is Tuesday today' (and I understand English), I acquire the belief that you are telling me that it is Tuesday today. I do not infer from your words that this is what you mean; rather, I simply acquire the belief that you are telling me this. Telling is an intentional act, an act which the teller means to do; that is, the teller has the intention of causing me to believe what he or she says by making the words come out of his or her mouth. Although testimonial beliefs are beliefs about what we are (in a wide sense) perceiving, I am classifying them as a separate kind of basic belief because—in virtue of the fact that we normally believe what people tell us—they are the indirect source of so much of our knowledge of the world beyond the very limited knowledge of what we perceive for ourselves. Telling may be done by writing, as well as by speaking; and I also count as a 'testimonial belief' the belief that the author of a book is telling us something, which we acquire when we read a purportedly historical book. So much of our general knowledge about the world arises from apparent memories that people have often told us so-and-so, although we cannot remember exactly who told us so-and-so on which occasions, and our believing what we are told. Our testimonial beliefs are the source of almost all our beliefs about science, history, or geography; and often we believe what we are told because we believe that our informants themselves believe what they are told, and that ultimately the chain of testimony goes back to the apparent memories of observers to have perceived certain events. We believe that people have told us that the world is several billion years old, that once upon a time Britain was a Roman province, or that Ankara is the capital of Turkey; and we usually believe what we are told about these matters, because we believe that the chain of testimony ultimately terminates in some true apparent memories.

Non-basic beliefs are ones which we hold because we believe them to be made probable by our basic beliefs.[1] Thus, by measuring the length and breadth of a room, I may acquire the basic belief that it is 7 metres long and 5 metres wide, and from that together with a basic belief which I already have that $5 \times 7 = 35$ I infer to a non-basic belief that it would need 35 square metres of carpet to cover the whole room. It seems to me that I acquire this non-basic belief because I believe that that belief follows from my basic beliefs. (The basic beliefs, I believe, give a probability of 1 to the non-basic belief; that is, they make it certain.) If I hear a knock at the door, I infer from that that someone is asking if they can enter the room, because it seems to me that 'there is a knock at the door' makes it probable that 'someone is asking if they can enter the room'. If I read in the newspapers that a man Kevin Stubbs, previously suspected by the police of being a contract killer, was seen at the place where a well-known politician was shot and killed and that the murder was committed by someone using a gun owned by Kevin, I acquire a basic belief that the newspapers contain these reports. This may lead me to form a non-basic belief that Kevin killed the politician. Then I acquire it, it seems to me, because I believe that the non-basic belief is made probable (though not certain) by the basic belief. Non-basic beliefs may interact with other non-basic beliefs or with new basic beliefs to form new non-basic beliefs or to eliminate old beliefs.

I now suggest that it is a fundamental principle of rationality, which I call **the principle of credulity**, that what seems probable is probable on the evidence that it seems probable, *given that there is no counter-evidence*; and we are right to believe (= it is 'rational' to believe; we are 'justified' in believing)[2] what seems probable *in the absence of counter-evidence*. This clearly applies to basic beliefs. We are obviously right to believe our experiential beliefs—that the tree is outside the window, that the telephone is ringing, that we are having the sensations which we seem to be having, and that '2 + 2 = 4'—in the absence of counter-evidence. These beliefs are probably true just because they seem to be true. The same goes for memory beliefs (our apparent memories); if I seem to remember that I had breakfast this morning, then I probably did have breakfast this morning. And the same goes for testimonial beliefs (the apparent testimonies of others); if it seems to me that someone who utters the words 'today is Tuesday' is telling me that today is Tuesday, then probably she is telling me that today is Tuesday. There is no other foundation for any of our beliefs than what seems to us to be the case as a basic belief. If we couldn't trust our basic beliefs in the absence of counter-evidence, we wouldn't have any grounds for believing anything. That is not to deny that sometimes some very quick glance at something or some rather faint apparent memory of something or a slightly inaudible apparent testimony may only make it mildly probable (= somewhat more probable that it is false than that it is true) that that something is so; and so we would need to look again in order to check out our first impression in order for it really to seem (= seem probable) that that thing is so-and-so in order to have a basic belief that it is so. But if, even after such necessary crosschecking, we could not trust our resulting basic beliefs in the absence of counter-evidence, we would have no foundation for any of our beliefs. The principle of credulity also applies to non-basic beliefs. If it really seems to me on the basis of what I read in the newspapers that Kevin killed the politician, and I have no other evidence about the matter, then surely I am right to believe that Kevin killed the politician.

Sometimes we need beliefs which are not just probably true, but very probably or almost certainly true; before a member of a jury finds Kevin guilty of murder, they need to believe that it is very probable ('beyond reasonable doubt') that Kevin murdered the politician. A belief that something is very probably true is a 'strong' belief that it is true. It follows from the principle of credulity that we are justified in believing that some proposition is very probably true if it seems to us that it is very probably true—in the absence of counter-evidence. I will call such a belief a 'strongly justified' belief. A basic belief will seem very probably true if it seems obvious to us that it is true—for example, that there are books in this room, or that I was talking to John two minutes ago. A non-basic belief will seem very probably true if it seems that it is made very probable by a strong basic belief (which might be the case, for example, if it seems to me that the basic belief is made probable by each of several different basic beliefs). I stress that the principle of credulity is always subject to the clause 'in the absence of counter-evidence'. I will discuss the role of counter-evidence shortly.

But first I need to make the point that having any belief commits one to a theory about what causes the belief. For beliefs, basic and non-basic, are by their very nature involuntary. Believing is something that happens to someone, not something that someone does. I believe that today is Monday, that I am now in Oxford, that Aquinas died in CE 1274, etc., etc. I cannot suddenly at a given time decide to believe that today is Tuesday, that I am now in Italy, or that Aquinas lived in the eighteenth century. I emphasize 'at a given time'. I can of course take steps to investigate whether my belief is true, and that may—or may not—lead to a change of belief. That we cannot choose our beliefs is a logical matter, not a contingent feature of our psychology. A 'belief' wouldn't be a belief if the believer chose to have it. For if having a belief that some proposition p is true was the result of a chosen action, then we would know that it was up to us (that is, depended on our choice) whether or not we would believe it. And then we would know that our belief that p was not acquired by a process likely to acquire the belief that p iff p is true; and in that case we would know that p was no more likely to be true than a random guess, and so we couldn't really believe it. For similar reasons we cannot believe that we believe p as a result of any process which would have operated whether or not p was true, for then also we would believe that it was improbable that that process would have produced a true belief, and so we could not really believe p. Rather, we must believe that what causes us to hold a belief that p is either the state of affairs believed (the event which p reports) or another belief which makes p probable and so constitutes evidence for p.

This clearly applies to basic beliefs. We believe that they are probably true, because we believe that they are caused by the states of affairs apparently believed. I couldn't believe that I was looking at a tree outside the window unless I believed that I was caused to believe this by the presence of the tree (via light rays reflected by the tree, impinging on my eyes). If I believed that I had chosen to 'believe' that I was looking at a tree, or if I believed that I was caused to believe this by being given a drug which causes a belief in the person who takes it to believe that he is looking at a tree, I would know that I had no grounds for believing that there was a tree outside the window, and so I wouldn't really 'believe' that I was looking at a tree. When we believe an apparent truth of reason, as a basic belief, we believe it because we believe that as we consider the sentence by which we hold it in our mind, that sentence being true causes us to believe that it is true—'it stares us in the face'. I couldn't believe that I remember seeing John in London yesterday unless I believed that my memory belief was caused by my perception yesterday of seeing John in London; and I couldn't believe that someone was telling me that John was in London unless I believed that his intention to tell me this caused the words to come out of his mouth.[3]

It also applies to non-basic beliefs. We believe non-basic beliefs because we believe that they are caused by the other beliefs which make them probably true. I couldn't believe any proposition on the ground that it was made probable by other beliefs if I also believed that I had chosen to adopt the resulting belief by a voluntary act of will. Nor could I believe it if I also believed that I was caused to believe it by any process independent of my will which would have operated whether or not the belief was true. I need to believe not merely that I am caused to hold the later belief, but that it is the earlier beliefs which cause me to hold the later belief because they make it probable. It may sometimes be up to me to choose whether to investigate what follows from some earlier belief of mine, but which conclusion I reach on the basis of my investigation is not up to me. I couldn't consciously reflect on—that is, bring to consciousness my beliefs about—all the evidence in favour of the Theory of Evolution by natural selection: the evidence of gradual changes in the forms of fossils in succeeding geological layers, of homologies of anatomical form between different kinds of animals, of geographical distributions of kinds of animals, of the results of breeding animals for various characteristics, and so on, and then decide whether or not to believe that the theory is true. I could decide to assume that the theory is true for some purpose (for example, in order to work out the consequences which would follow if it were true), I could decide to investigate the evidence more thoroughly, I could even decide to try to brainwash myself over a number of weeks in order to get myself to believe it; but I couldn't decide there and then to believe it or not to believe it. Either I am moved by the evidence in the form of other consciously held beliefs to believe the theory, or I am not moved by the evidence to believe it (because I find myself believing that the evidence is not strong enough to make the theory probable). If I believe it because I believe that the evidence makes it probable, then I believe that I believe it because the evidence caused me to believe it.

All beliefs, however, are open to **counter-evidence** (= **defeaters**). There are two kinds of defeaters—undermining defeaters and overriding defeaters. **An undermining defeater** to a belief is one which undermines our grounds for believing it; it shows that the grounds did not occur or were not good grounds for the belief. An undermining defeater to a basic belief is one which shows that the belief had a quite different cause from the state of affairs believed. If, for example, I apparently experience hearing my telephone ring, and then I notice that the noise which I supposed to be caused by the telephone is in fact coming from the television set where someone is depicted as hearing a telephone ring, that constitutes an undermining defeater for my apparent experience. It doesn't show that my telephone was not ringing, but it does show that the noise was not evidence that it was, because the noise had a different cause. If Ann seems to be telling me that she saw John, and then a neuroscientist shows me how he controls the brain events which make the words come out of Ann's mouth, that does not show that she did not have the intention of telling me that she saw John, but it shows that my belief that she was telling me this was not caused by such an intention. An undermining defeater for a non-basic belief is one which shows that the basic belief from which we have inferred it is false or does not constitute good evidence for the non-basic belief. For example, if a detective believes that John murdered James because George testified that he saw John murdering James, evidence that George was nowhere near the place of the murder at the relevant time and so could not have seen John murdering James undermines George's evidence, and so the detective no longer has reason to believe that John murdered James. By contrast, **an overriding defeater** x for a belief y is new evidence (making it probable) that *y* is false. If I apparently remember seeing John in London last week, and then someone tells me that John was overseas last week, that constitutes an overriding defeater for my belief that I saw John in London last week.

The evidence constituting the defeater (overriding or undermining) must itself come in the end from our basic beliefs; that is, from apparent experience, memory, or testimony. This counter-evidence need not be direct evidence of the non-occurrence of the event or of the evidence for it—for example, in the form of apparent testimony that the testifier was not present at the site of the alleged event. It may instead be indirect evidence, in the sense that it may be evidence making probable a theory which has the consequence that the event or the evidence for it apparently experienced, remembered, or testified to couldn't have happened—for example, evidence supporting a theory that George was blind and so couldn't have seen what he claimed to have seen. But in that case that latter evidence must itself be provided by apparent experience, memory, or testimony. In this situation we have to weigh evidence from these three sources against other evidence from these same three sources. Such is the structure of rational belief.

C. Pure Mental Events Often Cause Other Mental Events

It is evident that we sometimes have strongly justified non-basic beliefs, for example about history or science, which we believe because they are made probable by our basic beliefs about the evidence. So it follows from the results of the previous section that in these cases we are justified in believing that our basic beliefs cause non-basic beliefs, and so that some mental events often cause other mental events—in the absence of counter-evidence.

Our beliefs which it seems to us cause us to form other beliefs might do this either by causing them directly (as in Diagram 1a) or by causing some brain event which in turn (often via other brain events) causes the subsequent beliefs (as in Diagram 1b).

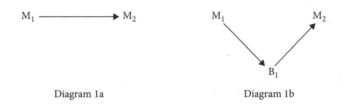

Diagram 1a   Diagram 1b

(In these and the subsequent diagrams in this chapter the 'M's represent mental events, and the 'B's represent brain events; events to the left of the diagram are earlier than events to the right, and arrows represent causal action. In the two above diagrams the 'M's represent beliefs.) In those cases where the later belief is formed immediately by an earlier belief and we are simultaneously conscious of both beliefs (as in my carpet example or when we work out from our beliefs about the cost of some individual purchases the total cost of the items purchased), it seems plausible to suppose that the final belief is reached by direct causation—as in Diagram 1a. But in the case of memory beliefs of experiences more than a few minutes earlier, where we believe some proposition because we believe that we had some past experience, for example I believe that John was in London yesterday because I apparently remember having seen him in London yesterday, the causation is fairly obviously indirect—as in Diagram 1b. We only seem to remember our experiences and actions of more than a few minutes earlier because of 'traces' of past events laid down in our brains, as is shown by neuroscientific evidence that brain damage of various kinds destroys the ability to recall past events.[4]

However, many philosophers and scientists hold that, while we may be unable to avoid believing that our basic beliefs cause non-basic beliefs (and that other mental events cause further mental events), this is an 'illusion of thought', and in fact no (pure) mental event (in my sense of an event distinct from a brain event) ever causes another mental event. These thinkers[5] normally claim that when it seems to us that a mental event M_1 causes another mental event M_2, what is really happening is that some brain event B_1 causes M_1 and at the same time B_1 causes a later brain event B_2, which causes M_2, and M_1 being followed by M_2 produces the illusion that M_1 causes M_2—as in Diagram 2.

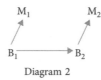

Diagram 2

On this account we never reach a conclusion (= acquire a belief that the conclusion is correct) as an effect of considering the evidence for it (= reflecting on beliefs that certain propositions reporting the evidence are true). Our beliefs that mental events often cause other mental events are strong beliefs apparently forced upon us by reflection on very many experiences of reasoning. If they are 'illusions', they are strong illusions. It follows from the results of section B that we need to have strong counter-evidence in order to be justified in deeming them unjustified. I now argue that it would never be possible for there to be such counter-evidence. Counter-evidence against the view that mental events often cause mental events would consist of evidence in favour of some scientific theory that when mental events (such as consciously held beliefs) seem to cause other mental events (such as other beliefs), these latter events are really caused not by mental events, but by brain events, in the way illustrated in Diagram 2. In order to establish this theory we would need to collect a lot of evidence of the following kind: whenever someone has a consciously held basic belief that a room is 7 metres long and 5 metres wide (M_{1a}) and a basic belief that $5 \times 7 = 35$ (M_{1b}), and then comes to have a new non-basic belief that it would need 35 square metres of carpet to cover the whole room (M_2), there is always a brain event (B_1) which both causes (M_{1a}) and (M_{1b}), and also causes another brain event (B_2) which causes M_2. And we would need evidence that this kind of connection holds without exception for many different kinds of mental events in many different kinds of people. Suppose I assemble evidence of this kind. Then that evidence would only justify me in believing that scientific theory if I believe that I am not choosing to believe that theory because I like thinking like this, but because I am responding to the consciously believed evidence, in other words that my beliefs about the evidence are causing me to believe that that theory is true. But then I believe that in this case some beliefs do cause another belief. So it would be self-defeating for me to believe that no beliefs ever cause other beliefs. What applies to me applies to anyone else who investigates for themselves whether beliefs cause other beliefs. And if anyone believes the theory that beliefs never cause other beliefs because some supposed expert tells them that he has concluded that that theory is true on the basis of evidence of the above kind, they would be justified in believing the expert only if they believe that the expert is himself justified in believing on the basis of his evidence that beliefs never cause other beliefs; and by the earlier argument that expert never could be thus justified.

D. Pure Mental Events Often Cause Brain Events

I now argue that it also follows from the results of section B that our intentions often cause brain events, and so pure mental events often cause brain events. Recall that by someone's 'intentional action' I understand an action which that person is intending to do; and by their 'intention' (= purpose) in what they are intending to do, I understand what they are meaning to achieve by what they are doing or trying to do. By a 'bodily action', I mean an intentional action which consists in causing some bodily movement. It often seems to us very strongly, as a strong apparent experience, that we perform intentional actions including bodily actions. I now argue that to perform a bodily action would be for our intention to perform the action, to cause the bodily movement. Consider first an intention which may or may not succeed in producing the intended effect—for example, suppose that I am trying to raise my arm when I am holding a weight; that is, to lift the weight. I may not succeed in lifting the weight, but if I do succeed, it seems to me strongly that it was me trying which caused the weight to rise, and so that lifting the weight was an intentional action. It seems to me strongly that this is so, because clearly the weight will not rise unless I try to raise it, and the harder I try, the higher it will rise. Most of our bodily actions are ones which are so easy for (most but not all of) us to perform and take so short a time that we are seldom aware of a time when we are trying to bring about the effect and have not yet succeeded in doing so. But clearly there is a difference between me intentionally raising my arm when I am not holding a weight and my arm just rising in a way unintended by me. That difference is that me intentionally moving my arm consists in me causing the bodily movement; that is, me having the intention to cause the bodily movement causing the bodily movement. Psychological studies of a kind that will be described in the next section show that even in such cases people are capable of distinguishing the time at which they formed the intention from the time when the movement began to occur. What goes for simple bodily actions caused by short-term intentions goes also, I suggest, for long-term intentional actions where someone's intention to pursue a long-term goal causes them to form the short-term intentions which cause the bodily movements necessary for that purpose.

So it often seems to us strongly that we form intentions which cause bodily movements. And when science makes it evident to us that all our bodily movements are caused more directly by brain events initiating sequences of events in our nerves which cause the bodily movements, it follows that it is very probable on the evidence of how things seem to us that our intentions cause the brain events which cause the bodily movements.

However, many philosophers and scientists claim that, while we may be unable to avoid believing that our intentions cause bodily movements, this too is an illusion of thought, and in fact no (pure) mental event (in my sense of an event distinct from a brain event) ever causes a bodily movement. We never do any action because we intend to do it. These thinkers normally claim that when it seems to us that some mental event M_1 causes some bodily movement which— we rightly infer—is caused more directly by a brain event, what is really happening is that some earlier brain event B_1 causes M_1, and B_1 also causes a sequence of other brain events (represented in Diagram 3b by B_2 and B_3) which in turn cause a brain event B_4, which causes the bodily movement. B_4 occurs later than M_1, and this produces the illusion that M_1 causes B_4—as in Diagram 3a.

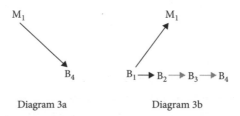

Diagram 3a   Diagram 3b

Then on this account our intentions never cause the intended bodily movements; both are caused only by brain events.

Since brain events often cause mental events, there is nothing inherently impossible in causation between such radically different kinds of thing. The only issue is whether in fact there is mental-to-brain causation. It follows from the results of section B that someone would only be justified in believing that mental events never cause brain events if they could produce counter-evidence to the well-justified strong belief that our intentions do cause brain events. I now argue that there could never be any such counter-evidence. Counter-evidence would consist of evidence which makes some scientific theory probable, from which it follows that mental events never cause brain events. We are never justified in believing some scientific theory unless we are justified in believing that that theory has made successful predictions or is a consequence of some wider theory which has made successful predictions. (An example of the latter is where we are justified in believing some theory about the path along which some distant star is moving, not because that theory itself makes successful predictions, but because it is a consequence of some general physical theory such as Newton's theory of gravitation that that star, having the particular mass and velocity it currently has, moves along a certain path.) So we need evidence of the occurrence of particular events and evidence that those particular events were predicted by the theory that mental events never cause brain events, or by a wider theory of which that narrower theory is a consequence.

The evidence that certain particular events occurred must come from apparent experience, apparent memory, or apparent testimony. It may seem to us that we are experiencing those events, or that we remember having perceived the events at some time in the past, or that someone is telling us that they have perceived those events. We have seen that when we believe apparent experiences, we believe them because we believe that the events apparently experienced are causing us to believe that we are experiencing them. If we didn't believe that there was this causal link, we would have no reason to believe that our apparent experiences of events provide us with any reason to believe that the events actually occurred. Our belief thus involves a brain event causing a mental event, which—we have seen—is a process of a kind which occurs frequently.

Likewise, when we believe an apparent memory of a past experience, we believe it because we believe that an apparent experience of a past event has caused the apparent memory of it. I pointed out earlier that where our apparent memories are memories of past experiences of more than a few minutes earlier, this must involve the past experience causing a brain event (a trace in the brain), and the brain event causing our subsequent apparent memory. It therefore involves a mental event (a past experience) causing a brain event in the way illustrated in Diagram 1b. (In future I shall count an apparent memory of a brain event less than a few minutes earlier as a case of apparent experience, because—possibly—our awareness of such an event may not involve mental-to-physical causation.) Again, if we didn't believe that there was this causal link, we would have no reason to believe that our apparent memories of events coincided with the actual occurrence of those events.

When we believe the apparent testimony of other people, we believe that our apparent experience of them telling us something has been caused by them telling us that thing, and so that their intention to tell us that thing has caused the words to come out of their mouth. If we also believe that the speaker intends to tell the truth, we will believe that his belief about what happened caused him to form the intention to tell us what he told us. So if I believe in the occurrence of some event because of someone's testimony that they perceived that event, I need to believe that the event caused an apparent experience of theirs (an uncontroversial brain-to-mental event causation), that that apparent experience caused an apparent memory (which will have involved mental-to-brain causation), and that an intention to tell the truth caused the apparent testimony (which also involves mental-to-brain causation). If I believe that John was in London last week because he seems to be telling me that he was in London last week, I need to believe that his being in London caused him to have the apparent experience of being in London, and that this caused his later apparent memory of having been in London (an instance of mental-to-brain causation), and that

that apparent memory together with an intention to tell me the truth caused the words 'I was in London last week' to come out of his mouth (another instance of mental-to-brain causation). If I didn't believe that these two mental-to-brain causal processes were occurring, I would have no reason to believe in the occurrence of the event which the speaker seemed to be telling me about. I conclude that while we may be justified in believing that some event which we are currently perceiving (or are otherwise experiencing) is occurring without supposing that any mental events cause brain events, it will only be rational of us to believe that some event which we apparently remember or to the occurrence of which someone else testifies occurred if sometimes mental events cause brain events.

Scientists rely totally on the consequences of the principle of credulity to determine what constitutes evidence for their theories. A scientist takes his apparent experiences—his observations and calculations—as probably correct in the absence of counter-evidence. Much scientific knowledge relies on apparent memory (e.g. of the results of experiments or calculations only written up later in the day). And all scientists rely almost all the time on the apparent testimony (written or spoken) of other scientists (and of themselves in their written accounts of their experiments and calculations) that they have had certain experiences (normally in the form of perceptions) and that they have done certain calculations. Science has no other source of evidence to support its theories; it is totally dependent on the apparent experiences, memories, and testimony of scientists. And the wider public relies totally on the apparent testimony of scientists with respect both to their experiences and to their calculations.

I argued that it follows from the principle of credulity that because it seems to us so strongly that mental events often do cause brain events, it is rational to believe that this is the case—in the absence of significant counter-evidence. This is a strongly justified belief, one very probable on the evidence that it does seem so probable. Counter-evidence would take the form of evidence supporting a theory that mental events never cause brain events. In order for us to be justified in believing that counter-theory, it would need, like any scientific theory, to make true predictions of events. We would need to learn about the occurrences of these events from apparent experiences, apparent memories, or apparent testimonies of their occurrences. A scientist could learn about the occurrence of an event by apparently experiencing it without any mental-to-brain causation being involved. But the only events about which she could learn in this way are events which were happening at or about the time of her apparent experience or memory of them. And even that scientist would not be justified at that time in believing that the counter-theory was true merely because of the occurrence of two or three events predicted by the theory. The scientist needs to know about more than a few successful predictions in order justifiably to believe some theory, and so she needs to know about the occurrence of events at other times. She could know about such events by relying on her apparent memory of having observed them in the past, or her apparent memory that a written record of the occurrence of those events was written by her and so constitutes her testimony to herself of the occurrence of those events. But to rely on apparent memory and testimony involves assuming that mental events cause brain events. So even the solitary scientist could justifiably believe that mental events do not cause brain events only by assuming that sometimes they do. Yet of course a solitary scientist would not really be justified in believing such a large-scale theory as that mental events never cause brain events without evidence about the mental and brain events of many different persons. In order to get that evidence, a scientist must rely on the apparent testimony of other observers that they apparently remember having perceived certain events. And so again she has to assume that sometimes mental events cause brain events. So any attempt to show that mental events do not cause brain events which relies on evidence about which mental events occur when, involves assuming that sometimes they do. Such an attempt is inevitably self-defeating.

E. The Libet Programme

The results of a recent neuroscience research programme, initiated by the work of Benjamin Libet in the 1980s, have been interpreted by many scientists as showing that conscious events (and so 'mental events' generally in my sense) never cause brain events. In the original and most influential Libet experiments[6] subjects were instructed to move their hand at a moment of their choice within a short specified period (for example, a period of 20 seconds). The subjects watched a very fast clock, and reported subsequently the exact time at which they formed their intention to move their hand. They reported the intention to move their hand occurring (on average) 200 msecs (milliseconds) before the time at which experimenters recorded the onset of activity in the subjects' muscles initiating the hand move-ment. (A millisecond is 1/1000 of a second.) Experiments of other kinds, Libet claimed, showed that subjects report the time of sensa-tions as occurring 50 msecs before the time of the brain events which caused them. That led Libet to hold that subjects misjudge the time of all conscious events by 50 msecs, and so he concluded that their intention occurred (on average) 150 msecs before the muscle activa-tion. However, electrodes placed on subjects' scalps recorded (on each occasion of hand moving) a build-up of electric potential, called 'the readiness potential' (RP), which was presumably caused by the occur-rence of a particular kind of brain event which occurred (on average) 550 msecs before the muscle activity and so 400 msecs before the occurrence of the intention. The last thirty years have seen very considerable progress in understanding the neural basis of intentional actions, made possible by new techniques which allow neuroscientists to identify far more precisely than by measurements of electric poten-tial on the skull which areas of the brain are active some exact number of milliseconds before the time at which subjects claim that they form some intention. The results of this work seem initially to give very considerable support to the view that a prior brain event of the kind which gives rise to RP is a necessary condition for the occurrence of a simple intentional bodily movement of the kind studied by Libet.

So, if the subjects' reports are at all accurate, there is this succession of events: a brain event followed by a conscious event (the intention), and also followed by other brain events and then (later than the intention) a brain event which directly causes the muscle activity and so the movement. Many neuroscientists have argued from this kind of evidence to reach the extraordinary conclusion that the intention does not cause the movement. Thus one group of neuroscientists concluded that Libet's data 'contradict the naïve view of free will—that conscious intention causes action. Clearly conscious intention cannot cause an action if a neural event that precedes and correlates with the action comes before the conscious intention'.[7] But that is a totally unjustified conclusion. Turning a light switch may 'precede and correlate with' the room being illuminated by a light, and turning the light switch comes before the passage of an electric current down the wire to the light, but that does not show that the passage of the electric current to the light does not cause the illumination of the room. One event X may cause another event Z by causing an event Y which causes Z. So it is equally compatible with all the data showing the correlation between an earlier brain event (B_1), the intention (M_1), and the brain event (B_4) which causes the movement, and also the most natural explanation of those data, to suppose that B_1 causes (in the sense of being a necessary part of the cause of) the intention (M_1), and that the intention causes the brain event (B_4), which directly causes the movement. Despite this obvious point, many neuroscientists prefer the rival explanation that an earlier brain event (B_1) causes both the intention (M_1) and (in parallel) a sequence of brain events leading to B_4 which causes the bodily movement without the intention causing any brain event (as illustrated in Diagram 3b).

Even if these experiments show that in the particular circumstances of the experiment a brain event B_1 causes a sequence of brain events which is a necessary part of the cause of an apparently intentional bodily movement, that wouldn't show that the intention was not also a necessary part of the cause. To show that, you would need to show that B_1 causes the very same sequence of brain events with or without subjects having the requisite intention (to produce that bodily movement).

M_1 (intention)   and also   no M_1 (no intention)

$B_1 \rightarrow B_2 \rightarrow B_3 \rightarrow B_4$ → hand movement $B_1 \rightarrow B_2 \rightarrow B_3 \rightarrow B_4$ → hand movement

Diagram 4a   Diagram 4b

(As in the earlier diagrams, the left to right direction of events in the diagram represents the past to future direction of time, and the arrows represent causation.)

Thus if—as Diagrams 4a and 4b illustrate—the latest brain event (B_4) causes a hand movement, and it could be shown that the same sequence of brain events always occurs after B_1, whether or not the subject forms an intention to move her hand (M_1) at some time after the first brain event and before the last brain event, that would show that the intention does not cause any of the brain events, and so does not cause the hand movement.

But the major problem with Libet-type experiments is that they rely on the apparent testimony of subjects for information about the time of the occurrence of their mental events. They are right to rely on this apparent testimony if they are right to believe that the subjects' past intentions to move their hand caused their later belief that they had that intention when the clock was recording (for example) 7.1 seconds after the beginning of the experiment, and their intention to tell this to the experimenters caused the words 'I formed my intention at 7.1 seconds after the beginning of the experiment' to come out of their mouths. Their original intention to move the hand may have caused their later belief that they had that intention without any mental-to-brain causation being involved (because the time interval is very short and so the causal process might be an instance of direct mental-to-mental causation). But their intention to tell us this causing the words to come out of their mouth is an instance of mental-to-brain-causation. So all Libet-type experiments designed to show that mental events do not cause physical events require the experimenter to assume that sometimes mental events do cause physical events. Such experiments might serve to show that certain kinds of bodily movement (for example, those studied in Libet-type experiments, or—more obviously—some very quick reactions such as jumping out of the way of a passing car) which we might regard as formed by our intentions are in fact not formed by our intentions. But they could only show this if we assume that other bodily movements (such as the movements of our lips in telling us about our intentions) are formed by our intentions.

Clearly the same general objection applies to any attempt to show that mental events do not cause brain events which relies on evidence about which mental events occur when. We could only get enough evidence to show the theory to be true by relying on the apparent testimony of other people, and that involves assuming that that theory is false. The view that mental events do not cause brain events follows from a more general doctrine popular among scientists and philosophers called 'the causal closure of the physical' (CCP). Since by far the most plausible example of mental events apparently causing brain events is the example of intentions apparently causing brain events, if it could be shown that intentions do not cause brain events, that would be very strong evidence in favour of the causal closure of the physical. However, for the reasons which I have given, this could never be shown by relying on evidence provided by subjects about their mental lives.

But could not CCP, and so the theory which follows from it that mental events do not cause brain events, be established on the basis of evidence merely about which physical events occur when, without relying on any evidence about which mental events occur when? Could not observation merely of physical events provide us with a justified belief in some very general deterministic physical theory from which it follows that every physical event has another physical event as an immediately prior necessary and sufficient cause? If so, it would follow that no brain event could have a mental event as a necessary part of its cause. For if a deterministic physical theory of this kind were true, the physical event would have occurred anyway;

whatever mental events the subject had could have made no difference to the brain events. Suppose that scientists discover that for each physical event F studied in large samples of many different kinds of physical events, there is some other immediately prior physical event E which a certain deterministic theory predicts will have F as its immediate effect. That would seem to be powerful evidence in favour of that theory and so in favour of CCP. The currently best established relevant physical theory, Quantum theory, is not—on the normal interpretation of that theory—a deterministic theory. It is compatible with Quantum theory to suppose that physical events do not fully determine succeeding physical events, and so Quantum theory does not rule out mental events sometimes making a difference to brain events. Nevertheless, it might be shown that Quantum theory is a quasi-deterministic theory in the sense that it follows from Quantum theory that the brain is so nearly a deterministic system that there is virtually no scope for our intentions (or other mental events) to make any significant difference to what happens in our brains, and so to which actions we perform. Would that not constitute powerful evidence in favour of the theory that mental events virtually never cause brain events?

The problem, however, remains that our evidence about which physical events occur when in these large samples of events must come from the reports of scientists about the results of their experiments; that is, from the apparent testimonies and memories of scientists about what they claim to have perceived. But we have seen that we are only justified in relying on apparent memory and testimony if we are justified in assuming that past observations cause brain traces which cause present memories and that people's intentions cause words to come out of their mouths. So again relying on the evidence of the apparent memory and testimony of scientists about what they have observed already seems to presuppose the falsity of CCP. Again, an individual scientist could believe that certain physical events are currently occurring on the evidence of his apparent experience of them—she could simply observe them without any mental-to-physical causation being required. But to get enough evidence to acquire a justified belief that the deterministic (or quasi-deterministic) physical theory is true, a scientist would require a lot more evidence than evidence about which physical events she had observed within the previous few minutes. And she could not get any more evidence unless she assumed the falsity of CCP. So there could not be a justified belief in any deterministic or quasi-deterministic physical theory and so in CCP, merely by relying on observations of physical events.

And even if there is some way in which a scientist could come to learn about which physical events had occurred in distant places at distant times without presupposing mental-to-physical causation,[8] they would need—if the occurrence of these events is to constitute evidence for a deterministic (or quasi-deterministic) physical theory— to have a justified belief that their theory predicts these events. Someone will have needed to calculate that the theory makes these predictions. What makes someone's belief that the theory predicts certain events justified is (if it can be had) experience (of oneself apparently currently 'seeing' that the calculations are correct, as an apparent truth of reason), a-memory (of having made the calculations in the past), or apparent testimony (from oneself or others that they have made the calculations). Apparent experiences, memories, and testimonies are mental events which the scientist needs to know about in order to know that her calculations are correct. And if a scientist could be consciously aware of all the calculations at one time, then indeed they would be justified in believing that the theory does predict the observed events, and so would be justified in believing the theory. Alas, for any scientific theory of any complexity, most experts at the centre of the field will be unable to be conscious over a short period of time of all the relevant calculations. Even as a scientist reads through the text of her calculations, she depends on her apparent memory towards the end of the calculations for her belief that the initial calculations were correct. Later in life all that she may a-remember is that it did seem to her earlier that the theory made those predictions. She may have a diary in which she recorded this, which will be her testimony about this to herself and others. Non-scientists and scientists less central in the field will depend on the testimony of those whom they regard as experts that they have made those calculations. So even if it could be established which physical events occurred when without relying on mental-to-physical causation, in order to be justified in regarding those physical events as evidence for a scientific theory, a scientist must rely on her memory of having made calculations or the testimony of others that they have made calculations showing that that theory predicted those events. And all non-scientists must rely on the testimony of scientists that they have made the relevant calculations. And so to have a justified belief that some scientists did make these calculations would involve presupposing that mental events cause physical events, and so presupposing the falsity of CCP.

My overall conclusion is that we are well justified in believing that mental events often cause physical events in the absence of counter-evidence; and that there could not be any counter-evidence of any significant amount. If current physical theories do not make space for mental-to-physical causation,[9] then they must be amended to allow for it if they are to provide a well-justified theory of the physical world. So, given that—as I argued—mental events are events in souls, we are well justified in believing that souls cause brain events, as well as that brains cause events in souls.

The fact that each human soul interacts with a brain enables us to answer the question whether it has a location. Larger physical substances occupy places in the sense that they exclude other larger substances of the same kind from a place; a table or a chair occupies a place because no other table or chair can be in exactly the same place as it is. Clearly a soul does not occupy a place in that sense; there is no region of space which it fills and from which it excludes any other souls or indeed any other substances at all. But a substance which does not occupy a place in this sense can be said to be located at the place if there is a place at which and only at which it exercises its causal influence, and by events at which it is itself causally influenced. In this sense a soul is located at that region of the brain with which it interacts and so is extended, although necessarily indivisible. If the soul ceases to be capable of interacting with its brain, and there is no other physical substance with which it is capable of interacting, then—even if it continues to have a mental life—there seems to be no sense in which it would have a location.

7

Could Science Explain Souls?

A. Cartesian Substance Dualism and the Evidence for It, Summarized

In previous chapters I have argued in favour of a version of 'substance dualism', understanding by 'substance dualism' any theory that each human consists of two parts—a soul (a pure mental substance) and a body (a physical substance). Our soul and body interact—some of our brain events cause events in our soul (pure mental events), and some events in our soul (pure mental events) cause brain events. I began my defence of this view by advocating the simple theory of personal identity—that being the same person as an earlier person is not to be analysed in terms of the later person having a body or brain or physical or mental properties (such as a-memory and character) continuous with those of the earlier person. It then followed that if some later person (for example, Alex) had properties (mental and physical) having a certain limited degree of continuity with the properties of an earlier person (Alexandra), and a certain limited amount of the earlier person's (Alexandra's) brain, it was still logically possible that the later person (Alex) was the same person as the earlier person (Alexandra), and also logically possible that she was not the same. I then argued—by means of the principle of the identity of composites—that if the later person (Alex) was in fact the same as the earlier person (Alexandra), there must be something about Alex which made her the same as Alexandra, which she would not have if she was not Alexandra. But as Alex could have all the same properties (mental and physical) and all the same physical parts (body and brain parts) whether or not she was Alexandra, she must have a pure mental part which I call a 'soul', which would make all the difference. She is Alexandra iff she has Alexandra's soul, and she is not Alexandra iff she does not have Alexandra's soul. I then defended a modified version of Descartes's argument for the soul, which yields the result that a person continues to exist iff her soul continues to exist, whether or not she has a body. In practice we can distinguish between actual souls by the body to which—contingently—they are connected. Your soul is the one that interacts causally with your body; and my soul is the one that interacts causally with my body. But each person's soul has a thisness; it is the soul it is quite independently of its properties (including the property of being connected to a particular body); and—it is logically possible—instead of the actual soul connected to my body, there could be any one of an infinite number of different actual or possible souls connected to that same body.

Theories of human nature other than substance dualism deny the possibility of the occurrence of phenomena which we can all recognize. In claiming that the only events are physical events, physicalism denies that there are pure mental events—that we have sensations, thoughts, etc. which are different from and do not supervene on the publicly observable brain (or other physical) events correlated with them. It thus fails to recognize evident phenomena. Mere property dualism acknowledges that there are pure mental events different from and not supervenient on brain events, and it may also allow that they interact with brain events. But it too fails to recognize evident phenomena. It is a phenomenon evident to me that I, who identify myself as the actual person who is in fact aware of having a certain mental property (but could—as I argued in Chapter 5—be having a different mental property instead), am in causal interaction with a particular identifiable body—let's call it B_s. It is a phenomenon evident to you, who identify yourself as the actual person who is aware of having a certain different mental property (but could be having a different mental property instead), are in causal interaction with a different particular body—let's call it B_y. Obviously the world would be different if I was in causal interaction with B_y and you were in causal interaction with B_s; and if I had had the mental life (the succession of all the past and present pure mental events) which you have had, and you had had the mental life which I have had. Yet if mere property dualism were true and so mental properties were properties of bodies or brains, and there were no souls, there would be no difference between these different situations, since the same mental lives would be associated with the same brains (and so bodies) in both situations—as depicted in Diagram 5. There is the objection to this view that these phenomena—you and I having the mental lives which we do—are not evident phenomena since we do not know to what we are referring when we refer to 'I'; that is, in my terminology, 'I' is not an informative designator. I rejected this objection in Chapter 5, and showed that 'I' is an informative designator and so these phenomena are evident phenomena.

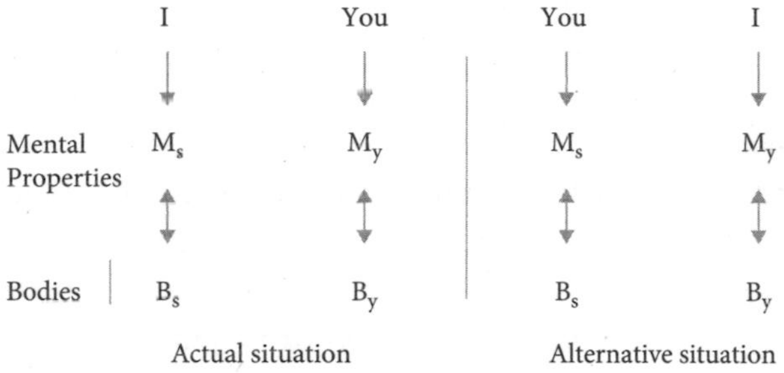

Diagram 5

Both you and I can recognize what the actual situation is and see that it is different from the alternative one. Only substance dualism can acknowledge that there exists this evident recognizable difference. All rival theories have the manifestly false consequence that there is no difference between these two alternative situations. It is therefore the only theory which is compatible with all the evident phenomena, and so is the only truly scientific theory. Hence theories rival to substance dualism are to be ruled out—on scientific grounds. I have argued in favour of the Cartesian, as opposed to the Thomist, version of substance dualism on the grounds that it is logically possible for each of us to exist without any body.

B. When Does a Human Soul Begin and Cease to Exist?

All that the arguments of this book have shown so far is that each human at each moment has a soul which makes them who they are; and that he or she continues to exist iff their soul continues to exist. I have not yet discussed when a soul (and so a human being) begins to exist, what reason there is for supposing that the same soul normally continues to be connected to the same body, and when a soul ceases to exist. Nor have I discussed whether organisms other than humans have souls. On all of these issues, I can provide only inductive probabilistic arguments—that is, arguments which show that given certain evidence, a certain view is probably true. And the only evidence I shall consider is evidence of the normal scientific kind about human and animal bodies and the mental lives associated with them. Different religions have different views about the beginning and end of human life. Many Eastern religions hold that our souls existed before our conception in a womb and so our birth is a reincarnation. Western religions—Judaism, Christianity, and Islam—deny reincarnation and claim that souls come into existence either at conception or at some later stage of the development of the foetus. And most religions hold that humans continue to exist after death; that is, after their bodies cease to function. And insofar as there is evidence in favour of the truth of one such religion (for example, in terms of miraculous events making it probable that the central doctrines of that religion have been revealed by God), and that religion teaches one of these views as a central doctrine, then that is evidence in favour of that view. But, as I wrote, in this book[1] I shall consider only evidence of the normal scientific kind about human bodies and the mental lives associated with them.

So when does a human begin to exist? A human being, on the definition I gave in Chapter 1, is a person belonging to a certain biological group, who has the capacity (or who will have the capacity as a result of normal developmental processes) to have conscious events of certain kinds. Neuroscientists are working hard to discover exactly what are the 'neural correlates of consciousness' in human brains, and as yet they have reached no agreed theory on this matter. But it would, I think, be fairly generally agreed that consciousness is caused by brain events interacting in a network of neurons constituting the cerebral cortex and thalamus. That network is in place in the brain of the foetus only by the seventh month of pregnancy.[2] So a reasonable guess as to when humans are first conscious is that it is around the seventh month of pregnancy. If souls exist before then, they are not conscious. If a human soul exists before the seventh month in connection with the body of a foetus, it does not manifest its presence and so we have no good reason to believe that it exists before then.

C. Is the Same Human Body Normally Connected to the Same Soul?

My arguments have the consequence that at every moment when there is a human being who is conscious or capable of being conscious, there is a soul connected with (that is, in continuing causal interaction with) that human's body. But why should we suppose that it is always the same soul which is connected to the same body during the course of the life of that body? Why not suppose that at each moment or perhaps on each new day, each body is connected to a different soul; and so—given, as I have argued, that it is their soul which makes a person who she is—each body is the body of a different person at each moment or on each day? On a physicalist theory an individual human being is the same substance as the body (or brain) which that human 'has'. But on a substance dualist theory soul and body (or brain) are disjoint—that is having a certain body (or brain) does not entail having a certain soul, and having a certain soul does not entail having a certain body (or brain), and so we need an argument to show that, at any rate normally, the same body is correlated with the same soul, and so the same human continues to have the same body during the life of that body.

While every conscious event lasts for only a very short time (the 'specious present') of perhaps a second or two, conscious events often overlap. That is, during the second half of some conscious event there occurs, co-experienced with it, another conscious event which continues after the first conscious event has ceased. For example, I may have a pain which lasts for one second; halfway through that pain I may have a thought which lasts for a second, including the half-second when I no longer have a pain, and before that thought has ended I may have an auditory sensation which continues after the thought has ceased; and so on. Co-experienced events are events experienced by the same person and so the same soul. Hence a continuing stream of overlapping events, constituting a stream of consciousness, must belong to the same soul and so to the same person. But the existence of a stream of consciousness will only guarantee that the same soul lasts for as long as that stream lasts; and we have no good reason to believe that any such stream continues for the whole time we are asleep.

I now claim that there are two kinds of good inductive reasons—that is, reasons which make it probable—that normally the same soul is connected to the same brain and so the same body, not merely for a waking day, but throughout the life of a human body—given that the matter and organization of its brain changes only very gradually. The first kind of reason is that normally each of us can a-remember very many previous conscious events caused by the same brain. As I argued earlier, if we cannot trust our own or someone else's a-memories, we can have no well-justified beliefs about the past; but surely obviously we do have well-justified beliefs about the past, and so it is rational to trust our a-memories. The content of those a-memories of each of us about our conscious events is not just that certain conscious events occurred, but that 'I' had these events; they concern my experiences, which public evidence shows to have been the experiences of a person who had a certain brain, and so a-memory is strong evidence for the same soul being connected to the same brain over time. The second kind of reason is that a person who has a certain brain has many of the same beliefs and desires as the earlier person who had that brain, or beliefs and desires resulting from gradual additions to or replacements of those ones—unless, of course, there has been some large, sudden change in the matter or organization of that brain. Mental properties, such as beliefs and desires, I argued earlier, are properties of souls. It is a simpler hypothesis to suppose that the same brain sustains similar beliefs and desires in the same soul at a later time than to suppose that it sustains similar beliefs and desires in a new soul at each period of time. The simplest hypothesis among hypotheses which lead us to expect the same phenomena on the same evidence is always more probably the true one.[3] To suppose that there is a succession of different souls connected to the same brain, each of which has largely the same beliefs and desires, would be to 'multiply entities beyond necessity'.

These two pieces of evidence—the existence of very many later a-memories of one's own earlier conscious events connected to the same (brain and so) body, and the continuity of the beliefs and desires of the later person with those of the earlier person with the same (brain and so) body—are good evidence that the two persons, and so their souls, are the same. But there are odd circumstances where there is no evidence of these kinds that the same body remains the body of the same person, but rather evidence pointing in the direction of a hypothesis that a different person from the earlier person with the same body has taken control of a whole particular brain or of one hemisphere of that brain.

The evidence which might suggest that sometimes a different person takes control of a certain body (and so of its brain) is provided by is some well-documented cases of **'multiple personality disorder'** (now often called 'dissociative identity disorder') when, during some periods of time, a subject (in the sense of whoever has a certain body and brain) has a certain personality (= character)—that is, certain general beliefs and desires—and during other periods of time (although having the same body and brain) has a quite different personality, not resulting from gradual changes of the normal kind in the earlier personality. When she has the former personality, she remembers all the events of earlier periods when she had that personality as events which 'she' experienced, and remembers none of the events experienced when she had the latter personality. When she has the latter personality, she remembers all the earlier events which 'she' experienced when she had that latter personality, but none of the events experienced when she had the former personality. However, I suggest, that while these cases could be interpreted as cases where different persons (and so different souls) control the same brain at different times, they are probably best interpreted as cases of 'representational disunity' (having parts of one's mental life not integrated with other parts of it). This means that the one body and so brain belongs to one person and so is connected to one soul, but a soul which thinks in one way and remembers past events of one kind during one period of time, and then thinks in a different way and remembers past events of a different kind during a different period of time. The argument for this interpretation of the data is that some 'personalities' don't last very long and show some recognition of the other personality, and that these cases are extreme forms of what some more ordinary humans are aware of in themselves. When their attitude to life changes, some more ordinary humans are willing to acknowledge only some of their past experiences which fit in with their present attitude.[4]

As well as these cases where—it might initially seem—a new person has taken control of a certain whole brain and so body, there are cases of a different kind where it seems as if a new person has taken control of some of a brain and thereby some of a body, leaving a different person (who may be the person whose body it was previously) in control of the other part of the brain and so of the other part of the body. I discussed earlier how we should interpret the results of 'anatomical hemispherectomy', where one cerebral hemisphere is removed. A less destructive operation, called a 'functional hemispherectomy', which is used to cure epilepsy in some less severe cases, is to cut the corpus callosum, the main bundle of nerves joining the two hemispheres, thus preventing the spread of epileptic seizures from one hemisphere to the other. Subjects without a corpus callosum, either as a result of this operation or born without one, are said to have a **'split brain'**, as a result of which they show some odd behaviour.

Before I describe this behaviour, I should explain that in all humans some afferent nerve impulses (including those from the right-side limbs and right sides of the two eyes) go in the first instance to the left brain hemisphere; and some impulses (including those from the left-side limbs and the left sides of the two eyes) go to the right brain hemisphere; and neural events in the left hemisphere are the direct causes of the movements of right-side limbs, and also normally of speech; and neural events in the right hemisphere are the direct causes of the movements of left-side limbs. In a normal brain (that is, one which is not a 'split brain') the 'signals' reaching one hemisphere are immediately transmitted to the other hemisphere, and the 'instructions' given by one hemisphere are immediately copied to the other hemisphere, all mainly via the corpus callosum.

The odd behaviour exhibited by those with 'split brains' was originally discovered by R.W. Sperry in the 1960s, and his work on the effects of split brains was developed by other neuroscientists in subsequent years. What they discovered was that those without a corpus callosum manifest awareness of stimuli presented to the left visual field only by means of bodily organs controlled by the right hemisphere, for example by movements of the left hand; and manifest awareness of stimuli presented to the right visual field only by means of bodily organs controlled by the left hemisphere, and so normally by speech. Thus, suppose you present to one such 'subject' a tray containing miscellaneous items and ask her to pick out those described on cards presented to her. Among the items on the tray are a key, a ring, and a key ring. You present to her the card reading 'KEY RING', but in such a way that the first word 'KEY' is visible only to her left visual field, and 'RING' is visible only to her right visual field. She then ignores the key ring, but picks out the key with her left hand and the ring with her right hand.

One interpretation of these phenomena is that 'split-brain' subjects have 'phenomenally divided consciousnesses', in effect two separate 'consciousnesses', each dependent on a separate brain hemisphere, one consciousness consisting of one set of conscious events and in control of one range of bodily movements, the other consciousness consisting of a different (but largely qualitatively similar) set of conscious events and in control of a different range of bodily movements. Sperry took that interpretation further by interpreting the phenomena as showing that in those without a corpus callosum there are two separate 'minds', so that even in the less influential hemisphere 'we deal with a second conscious entity that is characteristically human';[5] and so—although Sperry didn't express it in this way—he held that the two hemispheres are the hemispheres of two separate persons. Then, given my arguments of the previous chapters, it would follow that each hemisphere was connected to a different soul. If that is indeed the case, it would seem to follow that those 'subjects' who never had a corpus callosum were really two persons (each with a separate soul) all their lives; and that in those whose corpus callosum was severed some time later, at least one new person and so one new soul was created by the operation. But there are other interpretations of the condition of 'split-brain subjects'. One interpretation is that the subject has only one consciousness which interacts with the left hemisphere; the severing of the corpus callosum has the effect that many of his or her patterns of response (e.g. those of the left hand in typical split-brain experiments) are unconscious responses. Another interpretation is that there remains a single consciousness sustained by both hemispheres; and that the disunity of response is only 'access disunity'; that is, the subject is able to make responses of one kind only in reaction to information transmitted to one hemisphere, and responses of a different kind only in reaction to information transmitted to the other hemisphere. Yet another interpretation is Bayne's 'switch model', that consciousness in the split-brain person switches between the subject's two hemispheres.[6]

Each of these different interpretations of the 'multiple personality' and split-brain phenomena is compatible with the phenomena; but their advocates claim that their favoured interpretation fits the phenomena better; that is, it gives a simpler and so more probably true explanation of them. New observations may provide us with phenomena compatible with only some of these interpretations; but in the absence of such crucial phenomena, which interpretation is the most probable depends on which is the simplest and which makes the occurrence of phenomena of the kinds observed so far more probable than do other interpretations. As we have seen, one of the interpretations of split-brain phenomena is that in subjects without a corpus callosum each brain hemisphere is connected to a separate centre of consciousness and so—given my arguments—a separate soul. But in that case it might seem improbable that merely cutting the corpus callosum could create a new soul; and so it might seem to follow[7] that really each of the two hemispheres of every normal human body is also connected to a separate centre of consciousness and so a separate soul. On this view the nerve fibres connecting the two hemispheres, and principally the corpus callosum, ensure that the two souls always have mental events of exactly the same type—whenever one soul has a pain, the other soul also has a pain; whenever one soul believes that the Theory of Evolution by natural selection is true, so does the other soul.

However, I suggest, the existence of a few split-brain cases does not cast doubt on the fact that in all normal cases where there is a corpus callosum connecting the two hemispheres, it is very probable that the same one soul is connected to the same body throughout the life of the body. If normally there were two souls, each dependent on its own brain hemisphere, connected to the same body, we would expect that at least sometimes in all normal subjects limbs under the immediate control of one hemisphere would manifest different intentions from limbs under the control of the other hemisphere. For example, one limb would try to open a door and the subject would acknowledge the intention to do so by saying, 'I am trying to open the door', while the other limb would try to keep the door shut and the subject would acknowledge the intention to do so by writing with the left hand, 'I am trying to shut the door'. While there are sometimes conflicts between limbs in the split-brain patients in the weeks after surgery, the fact that there are not conflicts of this kind in normal humans is evidence that normally there is one and only one soul connected to one body. Also, there is evidence that subjects themselves deny that there are two of them sharing control of their body. And that might well lead us to prefer one of the interpretations of the split-brain cases which does not lead to the 'two souls' view.

D. When Does the Soul Cease to Exist?

I argued earlier that there is only evidence that there is a soul connected to a human body when it manifests its presence by that human's brain providing evidence that the human has the capacity to be conscious; and that there is no reason to suppose that the human exists when their brain shows no evidence of such capacity. So we may reasonably suppose that the continued existence of a human soul depends causally on the continued functioning of their brain. Hence, if my brain could be put into another body or into any other system which would keep it functioning, my soul would continue to exist. By the arguments of the previous section, it is very probable that a later brain very similar in its matter and organization or resulting from very gradual changes in its matter and organization (the pattern of interconnections between its constituent neurons) sustains the same soul as the earlier brain. And it is not at all probable that a later brain made of largely different matter organized in a different way would sustain the same soul. So any sudden replacement of most brain parts by parts from another brain or any sudden massive reorganization of brain parts (for example, neurons being broken down into their constituent atoms, and the atoms being rearranged into new neurons) would make it very probable that the brain has lost its connection with the original soul. So only if the brain matter is organized in somewhat the same way as in the earlier brain (for example, most of the neurons being made of the same atoms and being connected to other neurons in a similar pattern of intercon- nections) would we have strong reason to suppose that the later brain sustains the same soul as the earlier brain. Hence it seems to me only moderately probable that cryonics, the practice of freezing to a very low temperature the body of a person who has died from some disease, having made arrangements for the body to be unfrozen again when a cure for the disease has been found, would guarantee that that person would live again after their death. For while the process of brain freezing and unfreezing might preserve most of the neurons of the original brain, it would probably cause significant changes to the very precise distances between different neurons and so to the paths along which neural impulses would be transmitted. Such sudden changes of the previous brain organization would be expected to cause the resulting person have a very different character and different a-memories from those of the original person, as a result of which we would not have so much of our normal evidence for supposing that the persons are the same. So I conclude that it would be only moderately probable that even if there results from the unfreezing a subsequent normally functioning brain and so a conscious person, that unfrozen brain would sustain the same soul as the brain sustained before the freezing, and so the resulting person would be the same person as the pre-frozen person. But no scientific experiment could show conclusively whether an unfrozen brain is the brain of the same person as the person whose brain was frozen; all that we can say is that the greater the internal changes to the brain caused by the process of freezing and unfreezing, the more probable it would be that any resulting person would not be the same person as the original person.

But it is extremely improbable that 'downloading' a person's brain onto another brain or other system (for example, by 'teletransporting' it into the brain of some person on another planet) would preserve the original person and so their soul. (By a brain being downloaded onto another system, I mean its organization, its pattern of interconnections between separate units—in computer terms, its software— being installed in another system.) For my brain could be 'downloaded' many times onto different systems; and in that case since the systems onto whom my brain has been downloaded would all be different persons from each other, at most one of those persons could be me. And if the downloading was done a thousand times, the probability that any particular one of the resulting persons was me could be no greater than 1/1000. Now, suppose the downloading is done only once. The probability in this case that the resulting person is me cannot be affected by whether or not the process is repeated; mere repetition of the process cannot make any difference to who the first new person is. So since the probability would be very low if the process were repeated very many times, it must be very low even if it is not repeated. So downloading my brain organization onto some brain or system other than my brain is most unlikely to produce me.

So if a human being does not continue to live as a result of cryonics or some such process, what shows that they have lost the capacity for consciousness, and so they are dead? Until very recently humans were deemed to be dead when their hearts and lungs ceased to function and they could not be resuscitated, and in consequence they ceased to show by their public intentional bodily behaviour any awareness of anything happening in the public world. But it became possible in the 1960s to maintain a patient's respiration and circulation by 'extraordinary means of life-support'. If such patients continued nevertheless for a long time to be totally non-responsive to anything in the public world, they were said to be in a 'persistent vegetative state' (PVS). We have now learnt that some such patients have brain events of kinds which are correlated with conscious events in living non-PVS humans. This seems to constitute evidence that, although 'locked in' and unable to move their limbs, mouth, eyes, or any external part of their body, these patients are in fact conscious. A few such patients seem to have some brain events which are responsive to public events. For example, PVS patients were asked to imagine playing tennis or alternatively navigating around their own house, and then there occurred in the patient's brain events of the kind which occur in brains of non-PVS humans when they imagine themselves playing tennis or navigating around a house. Scientists used these results to develop what seemed to be a communication system in which PVS patients were asked to answer 'yes' to questions by imagining playing tennis and to answer 'no' by imagining navigating around their house. The questions which were followed in the patients by brain events of the kind normally correlated with playing tennis were questions to which those patients would have been expected to give the answer 'yes' if they were conscious and had a normal ability to speak; and the questions which were followed in the patients by brain events of the kind normally correlated with imagining navigating around a house were questions to which those patients would have been expected to answer 'no'. That seems to be very good evidence that such patients are conscious. However, even if someone is so locked in that they do not understand written or spoken commands, nevertheless they may still be conscious; and, I suggest, the mere fact that they have brain events of a kind that are correlated with conscious events in normal persons is significant evidence that they are conscious. But clearly when someone's brain largely ceases to function at all and this state seems permanent, the evidence strongly supports the conclusion that they are totally incapable of being conscious and so are dead. There are disputes yet to be resolved about just how much of the brain needs to cease to function for it to be almost certain that the person is incapable of being conscious ever again and so is dead; and so there are two different criteria of brain-death—the whole-brain criterion and the brainstem criterion— used as legal tests of death in different legal jurisdictions.[8]

On a physicalist view of humans, the capacity of a human to be conscious just consists in the functioning of their brain, and so—of logical necessity—when a human's brain ceases to function, that human ceases to exist.[9] On the substance dualist view, however, the dependence of the continued existence of the soul on the continued functioning of the brain which sustains it is only a causal dependence, not a logical dependence. It is logically possible that the soul could continue to exist when it is no longer sustained by its original body, and could then be joined to a new body. There would be such evidence for the continuing existence of a soul after death if it was a common occurrence for young children to apparently remember in much detail the life of some earlier person, now dead; and for those a-memories to be accurate memories of what that earlier person did and (as far as we can judge) experienced. For, as I argued in Chapter 6, by the principle of credulity we are always justified in trusting our apparent memories, in the absence of counter-evidence, and the accuracy of the apparent memories would provide some evidence available to others for believing the memories of the children. However, even if some young children did have a-memories of the lives of some previous person, the fact of non-continuity of their brains with those of the previous person must constitute counter-evidence to that claim. Whether the counter-evidence is strong enough to outweigh the positive evidence would depend on how many, how strong, and how accurate were the a-memories. However, insofar as there was a balance of evidence in favour of the young children being the same as the previous persons, that evidence would show that the soul of the previous person had survived death. Advocates of Eastern religions sometimes claim to have evidence of this kind; but I have not myself found it strong enough to outweigh the counter-evidence. Alternatively, as I mentioned earlier, there could be evidence for the truth of some metaphysical or religious system, such as the Christian or Islamic creed, that has as a consequence that souls continue to exist after the death of their body and are joined to new or revived bodies. But, to repeat, I shall not be discussing evidence of these kinds.

E. Could There Be a Scientific Explanation of the Existence and Life of the Soul?

Given what we reasonably believe about souls which I have described in sections A to D, could science explain the existence of souls and their causal connections with brains? A **scientific explanation** of some event E consists in adducing some initial event C (a cause) and a law or laws of nature L, such that the occurrence of E is entailed (or made probable) by {C and L}. A **law of nature** is a general principle which determines that all events of some type (that is, all events of substances having a certain collection of properties) cause (of physical necessity or with a certain physical probability) an event of some other type (that is, an event of a substance having a certain different collection of properties, or a substance of a certain type coming into existence or ceasing to exist). A simple example of a low-level scientific law would be 'all rotations of a coil of wire within a magnetic field cause the coil to have an electric current flowing in it at an immediately subsequent time'. Then there could be a scientific explanation of the event of a particular coil having an electric current flowing in it at a certain time t_2 by that coil rotating within a magnetic field (C) at a very slightly earlier time t_1, and the law (L) that 'all rotations of a coil of wire within a magnetic field cause the coil to have an electric current flowing in it at an immediately subsequent time'. Then {C and L} entail E, and so—given that C actually occurred and that L is indeed a law of nature—explain the occurrence of E. An example of a higher-level law of nature is Newton's law of gravitation: 'all physical substances having a mass m cause all other physical substances having a mass m' at a distance r from them to be attracted towards them with a force proportional to mm'/r^2 (at the same time)'. In most explanations in the physical sciences, the description of the initial event will be a detailed one and it may need quite a long deduction to show that the conjunction of the description of that event and several laws entail the occurrence of the event to be explained, but the pattern of explanation is the same as in my simple earlier example. Thus the positions of the planets today are explained by their positions, masses, and velocities and those of the Sun exactly a year ago (initial event), and the operation on them of Newton's laws (his three laws of motion and his law of gravitation). For it follows from Newton's laws that if there are one day bodies of the actual masses of the Sun and the planets with the velocities and positions relative to each other which the Sun and planets actually had a year ago, then exactly a year later there will be such bodies having positions relative to each other occupied by the Sun and planets today.

So if there is to be a scientific explanation for the coming into existence of human souls, there must be some law of nature of the form that 'all human foetuses at a certain stage of development cause the existence of a human soul' (at that or an immediately subsequent time) (for what that stage is, see section B). And if there is to be a scientific explanation of the continuing causal interactions between the brain and the soul, there must be innumerable laws about which brain events of which kind cause mental events of which kind (in the soul caused to exist by that brain), and which mental events of which kind cause brain events of which kind (in the brain which caused that soul to exist). Such laws together with the occurrence of foetuses having brain events of particular kinds and the humans into which they develop having brain events of the kinds that they do have would then explain the existence of souls and the mental events which occur in them.

Assuming for the moment that there is such a scientific explanation for the coming into existence of human souls by a law of the type described above, let us now consider whether there could be laws of nature that explain the continuing soul/brain interaction; that is, the brain event/mental event interaction. If there is to be a scientific explanation for this, there would need to be innumerable different laws. There would need to be brain-to-soul laws of the simple form 'all brain events of type B_1 cause a mental event of type M_1', or perhaps of a more complicated form such as 'all brain events of type B_1 cause mental events of type M_1 in souls which have such-and-such mental properties'. And there would need to be soul-to-brain laws of the simple form 'all mental events of type M_2 cause a brain event of type B_2', or of a more complicated form such as 'all mental events of type M_2 cause brain events of type B_2 in brains which have such-and-such brain properties'. In these laws the mental events would be events in that soul which was caused to exist by brain events in the brain in which B_1 and B_2 occur. So there would be a law determining that any brain event of one kind causes a red sensation, a law determining that any brain event of a certain other kind causes a thought that today is Thursday in souls which have beliefs about days of the week, a law determining that any brain event of a certain kind causes a desire to smoke cannabis, and a law determining that any brain event of yet another kind causes in souls who have certain beliefs about physics a belief that Einstein's Theory of Relativity is true. And there would need to be laws of soul-to-body causation such as a law that any mental event of a person's intention to move their arm causes a brain event in brains of a certain normal kind which then causes the arm of the human whose brain it is to move; and there would need to be a law that any person's intention to go to London, together with a belief that to go to London they need to go to the railway station, causes the motion of the legs of people whose brains have certain properties in the direction of the railway station. And so on, and so on.

It is plausible to suppose that there are such laws, for they would explain the otherwise inexplicable causal connections between our mental life and our sensory input and bodily behaviour. And indeed, scientists are beginning to discover statistical correlations between certain kinds of mental events and certain kinds of brain events.[10] It is not implausible to suppose that neuroscientists might eventually discover some more precise deterministic laws of these kinds. To discover such laws the scientists would need to study the brains of many humans who told investigators which mental event they were having when their brains were in such-and-such a state. To do that, scientists need to know what these humans mean by their descriptions of their own mental events. Humans may understand the words which occur in their descriptions of the content of their propositional events in different ways. Even a word describing a public object such as a 'table' may be understood by people speaking the same public language in different ways. Some English speakers count any flat surface supported by legs at waist height as a 'table', whereas others do not count a desk or a sideboard as a 'table'. Until investigators have sorted out what some speaker means by a 'table' they will not know what she means by her claim that 'it occurred to me that there was a table in the next room'. What someone means by a word applicable to a public object such as a 'table' should nevertheless be resoluble by asking them various questions about which objects they would call 'tables'; and so scientists could discover which mental event someone was having when they claimed that 'it occurred to me that there was a table in the next room'. But, as we saw in Chapter 5, we could never be more than moderately confident about what other people mean by their descriptions of the sensations they are having. And without having greater justification for our beliefs about what people mean by their descriptions of their sensations, we could only have limited justification for any claim about what are the laws determining which brain events cause which sensations. Further, mental events of most kinds differ in strength—one belief is stronger than another, one sensation is stronger than another; and yet there is no way of measuring the strength of someone's belief or sensation, except relative to some other belief or sensation of theirs. Someone can know and tell scientific investigators that some 'acute pain' of theirs is stronger than another pain which they have had; but there is no way for them to know or for scientists to discover whether that 'acute pain' is three times as strong or only twice as strong as some other pain of the same person, let alone of some pain of some other person. Measurement of the numerical value of a quantity of some property requires a public measuring rod or instrument of some kind to be put alongside the object whose property is being measured; but public measuring devices could not be put alongside a pure mental event. Public measuring devices can only measure physical events. For all these reasons it is very probable that scientists could discover only brain event/mental event and mental event/brain event laws of a rough approximate kind.

Further, it is very implausible to suppose that scientists could ever discover a general theory from which such detailed laws of soul/brain interaction as they could discover could be derived. They would be able to discover those laws for which they could find subjects who had a brain event of exactly the same type as each other and agreed in reporting a correlated mental event of the same type; and if they could discover many such subjects, they could reasonably suppose that the correlation which they had discovered constituted a law. What the scientists would then have would be like a list of phrases giving the equivalent in a foreign language of some English phrase, without a grammar and dictionary which would allow readers to discover the foreign language equivalent of some new English phrase. When scientists observed that someone had a brain event of a slightly different type from those studied previously, they could not infer from the list of correlations they had established which (if any) mental event that brain event of the new type was causing. They could only do that if they had a general theory of how differences in brain events lead to differences in mental events, from which they could derive many detailed laws including ones about the mental effects of brain events of types which they had not studied previously. Such a general theory would be like a grammar and dictionary of a foreign language from which readers could discover how to translate into that language some English sentence not previously translated.

My grounds for claiming that it is very implausible to suppose that scientists could ever discover such a general theory are the following. What makes a scientific theory such as a theory of mechanics able to explain a diverse set of mechanical phenomena is that the laws of mechanics all deal with the same sort of thing—physical substances, and concern only a few of their properties—their mass, shape, size, and position, which differ from each other in measurable ways. One substance may have twice as much mass as another, or be three times as long as another. In mechanical interactions between substances the values of these measurable properties of some substances are influenced only by the values of the same properties of other substances— for example, substances change their position and velocity when subject to forces originating from other substances in virtue of the positions, masses, and velocities of those other substances. Because the values of a few such measurable properties are influenced by the values of only a few other measurable properties, there are a few general laws which relate two or more such measurable properties in all physical substances by a mathematical formula. There is, for example, not merely a law that all events of a substance of 100 g mass and 10 m/sec velocity colliding with a substance of 200 g mass and 5 m/sec velocity cause such-and-such another physical event; and a quite unrelated law for what is caused by a substance of 50 g mass and 20 m/sec velocity colliding with a substance of 75 g mass and a velocity of 5 m/sec; and other unrelated laws for each different mass and velocity of colliding substances. There is a general law of the conservation of momentum that for every pair of physical substances in collision the quantity of the sum of the mass of the first multiplied by its velocity plus the mass of the second multiplied by its velocity is always conserved; and from that we can deduce the relative subsequent velocities of substances of masses and velocities never previously observed. There can only be such general laws because mass and velocity, being physical properties, can be measured on public scales—for example, of grams and metres per second. The same general point continues to hold when physics is extended to include a few more measurable quantities (charge, spin, colour charge, etc.) which interact with mechanical and electro-magnetic quantities, that we can construct a general theory of physics which entails more detailed laws about what happens in interactions of different kinds between substances having values of these quantities never previously observed.

Yet a soul/brain theory, a system of mental/physical laws, would need to deal with interactions between things of very different kinds from each other—physical substances and pure mental substances. Like other physical events, brain events differ from each other in the chemical elements involved in them (which in turn differ from each other in measurable ways) and in the velocity and direction of the transmission of measurable electric charge. But mental events do not have any of these properties. The propositional events (beliefs, desires, etc.) are what they are, and have the influence they do, in virtue of their propositional content. My intention to read a book is what it is because of what I understand by a 'book'; and my intention to go to bed is what it is because of what I understand by 'go to bed'. The difference between these two intentions is not analysable in terms of the one having a different location in space, or more or less of a few measurable quantities. The contents of person's propositional events differ from each other in the way that the meanings of different sentences of a person's language differ from each other, and these differences require the very large number of rules contained in a dictionary and grammar of the language to express them. These rules are independent rules and do not follow from a few more general rules. Only some of the words which occur in a dictionary can be defined adequately by other words in the dictionary; the meanings of many words are determined in large part by the examples to which they apply—in the way illustrated in Chapter 5. And there are many different ways described by the grammar of the language in which words can be put together so as to form sentences with different kinds of meaning. Mental events do not differ from each other in any measurable way, nor do they have any intrinsic order among themselves. So any soul-brain theory which sought to explain how brain events cause the beliefs, desires, etc. which they cause would consist of laws relating brain events having numerically measurable values of transmission of electric charge in various circuits, to beliefs, intentions etc. formulated in propositional terms and to sensations (none of which would be numerically measurable on public scales). So it looks as if the most that scientists could discover would be an enormously long list of separate laws relating brain events (of certain objective strengths) and mental events (of strengths measurable only relative to the strengths of mental events of the same person) without these laws being derivable from a few more general laws.

Laws of nature are what they are, independently of the process of evolution by natural selection of organisms best suited to survive. But natural selection could provide an explanation of why we have brains, events in which—in accordance with such laws—cause and are caused by the mental events which humans have. For example, we are more likely to survive if we have true beliefs about the presence of food, enemies, and friends rather than false beliefs about these matters, or no beliefs at all; and so natural selection can explain why we have sense organs which cause brain events of the kind which cause true beliefs about these matters rather than false beliefs or no beliefs—in accordance with already existing laws. And since we are more likely to survive if, in the light of such true beliefs, we form intentions of the kind which cause our bodies to make the movements which we believe will enable us to catch prey and escape predators, natural selection can explain why we have brain events which—in accordance with such laws—cause desires to form such intentions. And natural selection can explain why we have brain events of a kind caused—in accordance with such laws—by such intentions, and which cause the required bodily movements. But the fact remains that natural selection of systems of mental events conducive to survival requires there to be, antecedently to the operation of natural selection, innumerable brain/soul and soul/brain laws determining which mental events cause and are caused by brain events and other mental events, laws of a kind which natural selection could use to give a selective advantage to organisms with the right kinds of brains.

F. Which Non-Human Organisms Have Souls?

I argued in Chapter 2 that every animal who has the capacity for consciousness is a mental substance. The same arguments that I deployed in subsequent chapters to show that the mental substances who are humans have souls will show that those animals who are conscious also have souls. For the same issues arise with such animals as arise with humans, as whether an animal who is about to receive a substantial brain transplant will exist after the transplant, and so enjoy the good things which the subsequent animal will enjoy or suffer the bad things which the subsequent animal will not enjoy. And even if the animal itself does not have enough of a concept of the future to be able to desire to survive the transplant, the animal's owner may very well wish that his animal continues to exist and has a good subsequent life, and so will wish to know whether it is probable that the transplant operation will have that effect. Different theories of animal identity will have different consequences for whether the animal will survive the operation. And the same arguments against complex theories of personal identity, as that they are arbitrary and lead to irresolvable duplication, also count against complex theories of animal identity and so lead us to a 'simple' theory of animal identity, which in turn leads to the view that such animals have souls, and that their soul is what makes the animal the animal it is. Hence animals who have the capacity for consciousness are pure mental substances. A later dog is the same dog as an earlier dog iff they have the same soul. (So the name 'animalism' for the view described in Chapter 3, that a person is the same person as an earlier person iff they have the same body, is very misleading.)

The evidence that the higher animals are conscious is that their brains have regions very similar to the regions of human brains in which brain events of similar kinds occur, which—as far as we can judge at present—are the ones which give rise to conscious events in humans, and which are often followed by similar behaviour in animals to that by which the conscious events of humans are followed. For example, when humans touch a hot stove, that causes a brain event in them which causes them to feel pain, as a result of which they avoid touching that hot stove in future. If a gorilla touches a hot stove, that causes a brain event in him, as a result of which he avoids touching the hot stove in future. The overall similarity between the gorilla's brain and human brains gives us an initial reason to believe that the brain event which occurs in the gorilla is of the same kind as the brain event which causes pain in humans, and so probably causes pain in the gorilla. That it does so is then confirmed by the fact that the gorilla reacts to what has happened in the same way as humans do.

Conscious events in us are never caused directly by input to our sense organs, but only by the brain events caused by sensory input, nor do conscious events cause bodily movements directly, but only via the brain events which they cause; and we have no evidence that any physical events other than brain events cause or are caused directly by conscious events. So it is a mistake to argue, as so many psychologists do, merely from some organism having sense organs similar to ours which are sensitive to light waves, sound waves etc., and making bodily movements of a kind similar to those which we make in response to similar stimulation of those sense organs, that that organism is conscious. Unless an organism also has regions of a kind similar to those of our brain, in which events occur similar to our brain events which cause conscious events, we have no good reason to suppose that that organism is conscious. Its responses to stimulation of its sense organs may very well be totally non-conscious ones.

Hence if—improbably—it turned out that a gorilla touching a hot stove did not cause a brain event of anything like the same kind as that caused in humans, that would lead to considerable doubt about whether the gorilla felt any pain or any pain of the same kind as humans feel. (Of course, it is certainly logically possible that animals whose brains are very different from ours do feel pain, and that is why philosophers are right to take account of the problem of 'multiple realizability', discussed in Chapter 2.)

This pattern of argument can in principle be applied to the results of psychological research on animal behaviour and neurophysiology to reach some fairly probable conclusions about which animals are conscious and the kinds of mental events which different kinds of animal have. Or at least it could reach some such conclusions when we have a lot more results from such research. But the difficulty in reaching even fairly probable conclusions is that quite clearly consciousness depends on brain events over a wide area of the brain; and all animals, including even the great apes, have brains which are somewhat different from human brains. As animals cannot tell us anything about their conscious lives, all we can do is to construct the simplest and so most probable theory of which properties brain events need to have in order to cause and be caused by which mental events in humans, and then conclude from that theory that those animals in whom brain events have those properties are conscious. If that theory was much simpler and so much more probable than other rival theories, then it would follow that its consequences were probably true. Different scientists have produced very many rival theories about which properties of human brains are necessary for consciousness, and these different theories have different consequences for which other animals are conscious and which kinds of mental events they have. As yet, there is no theory of this kind on which most scientists agree.[11]

Still, all scientists agree that the similarities between the brain events in the higher animals and those in humans do make it very probable that the higher animals have mental lives to some degree similar to ours, from which it follows by my arguments that being conscious entails having a soul that those animals have souls on which those mental lives depend. It seems reasonable to suppose that all mammals (and possibly most other vertebrates) have sensations and simple intentions (to catch prey, escape from predators, mate, etc.), desires (of kinds which give rise to these intentions), and probably—in the case of the higher apes—occurrent thoughts (for example, it may suddenly occur to a gorilla who desires to get food out of its reach how to use a stick to reach it). But since the brains of invertebrates (insofar as they have brains) are of quite different construction from those of humans, it is not probable that they are conscious and so not probable that they have souls, even if they have sense organs sensitive to the kind of input to which our sense organs are sensitive and they make bodily movements somewhat similar to ours. But only if we had a general theory of the kinds of differences in brain events which cause different kinds of sensations and thoughts, of the kind which I argued we would be most unlikely to discover, would we be able to discover what kinds of sensations and thoughts animals have. For example, only with such a theory would we be able to discover (from an examination of their brains) what kinds of auditory sensations bats have indicating to them the presence of other objects, instead of the normal kinds of visual sensations by which other mammals detect other objects.[12]

If scientists were able to discover, on the basis of their studies of human brain events and their connections with mental events, a probably true theory of which properties brain events need to have in order to cause and be caused by mental events, that theory might or might not be such as to enable us to draw consequences about whether beings of kinds other than humans and the higher animals are conscious and so have souls. If the laws of that probable theory turned out to be laws determining how all systems with a certain kind of central controlling part (with an architecture and so interconnections similar to those of our brains) are conscious, then it would follow that robots or beings on other planets made of quite different matter from ourselves but with a controlling part of that kind probably are conscious and so have souls. But if the laws proved to be laws determining only how systems formed of cells made of organic material with a nucleus having chromosomes made of DNA are conscious, then that theory would not make it probable that robots or beings on other planets made of quite different matter from us are conscious,[13] and so we would have no reason to believe that they are conscious. Whether we are justified in believing that there are laws of this latter kind will depend on the normal criteria mentioned earlier, for whether some set of postulated laws is probably true—that is, whether postulating such laws provides simpler and so more probable explanations of the available data. But inevitably a law of a narrower kind concerned only with animals having similar brains to those of humans will be much more probable than a much wider law concerned with all systems having a similar architecture, which entails the narrower law. (This follows from the probability calculus. But it is in any case obvious from the fact that the more you claim, the more likely it is that you will make a mistake; and so it is more likely that a theory about all systems will be mistaken than that a theory entailed by the former theory about a small class of those systems will be mistaken.) Hence it is much more probable that the higher animals are conscious than that robots made of quite different material are conscious.

Medieval thinkers, following Aristotle, thought that there were souls of three kinds—'nutritive souls' (possessed by organisms such as plants which ingest food and grow), 'sensitive souls' (possessed by organisms such as animals which, as well as ingesting food and growing, are conscious), and 'rational souls' (= 'intellectual souls') (possessed by organisms such as humans which can reason). Thomas Aquinas, following Aristotle, held that for the first period of human pregnancy, the foetus has a nutritive soul, for the second period it has a sensitive soul, and only later in pregnancy does it have a rational soul; and so only later in the pregnancy is a human foetus a human being.[14] So my view expressed earlier in this chapter, that persons and so human beings come into existence only in the later stage of pregnancy, was shared by Aristotle and Aquinas. (On my account of a soul as a pure mental substance, Aquinas's 'nutritive soul' is not a soul in my sense, because there is no reason to believe that plants and any similar organisms are conscious and so have 'souls' in my sense.)

G. The Limit to Scientific Explanation of Souls

There is, however, one aspect of soul/brain interaction for which there could never be a scientific explanation. I wrote earlier that 'if there is to be scientific explanation of the coming into existence of human souls, there must be some law of nature of the form that "all human foetuses at a certain stage of development cause the existence of a human soul"', and I made the temporary assumption that there must be such a law. The problem is, however, that any such law could never explain which particular soul any particular human foetus causes to exist. For, as we saw earlier, laws of nature are principles which determine relations between substances which depend on their properties; they determine that all events consisting of a substance having a certain conjunction of properties cause an event of that substance or a substance related to it in certain ways to have certain properties, or cause the existence of a substance with certain properties, or cause a substance with certain properties to cease to exist. Particle physics has discovered many laws of the form that events of certain kinds cause the existence of certain new particles. For example, there is a law that all free neutrons decay (with high probability after some fifteen minutes) into a proton, an electron, and an antineutrino; that is, all events of freeing a neutron from being bound to any other particle causes the existence of a proton, an electron, and an antineutrino in the place previously occupied by the neutron. The law does not state which proton (electron, or antineutrino) neutron decay causes. But—on the assumption discussed earlier that fundamental particles do not have thisness— there would be no difference between one proton occupying a certain place and another proton occupying that place. Protons are the protons they are solely in virtue of their essential (intrinsic and relational) properties. So as a law can explain why a proton comes into existence with all its properties (including the property of occupying a certain spatial location), there is nothing left to be explained. But persons, I have argued, have thisness; that is, for any person having any particular conjunction of intrinsic and relational properties, there could—it is logically possible—exist instead of that person any one of innumerable different persons with exactly the same (intrinsic and relational) properties. So while there could be a law determining that all foetuses whose brains have certain physical properties cause the existence of *a* soul with such-and-such mental properties, no law could determine which soul (and so which person) that would be. No law could have determined that certain events in the foetus in my mother's body would produce me rather than any of the innumerable possible duplicates of me.

Opponents of substance dualism claim that it is a difficulty, which they call 'the pairing problem', for substance dualism that it cannot explain why a particular brain is 'paired with' a particular soul. But, I would urge, given the—to my mind—very strong arguments in favour of the position that persons are the persons they are in virtue of their souls, and souls have thisness, it is inevitable that laws of nature could not explain this connection. For laws of nature do not concern individual things as such; they concern individual things only insofar as they have certain properties. If there were good reasons to suppose that fundamental particles have thisness (and, as I pointed out earlier, most physicists think that there are no such good reasons), it would not be a good objection to this theory that it left something inexplicable by laws of nature. Whether laws of nature can explain all phenomena or only most phenomena is a matter for scientific investigation, and not a presupposition of all investigation. A true scientific theory must be compatible with all observed data— and I argued at the beginning of this chapter that only substance dualism is thus compatible—but it may not be able to explain all observed data. The normal interpretation of Quantum theory, for which there are good reasons, claims that the movements of fundamental particles cannot be fully explained by laws of nature. Quantum theory can explain why a photon emitted from a light source goes through one of two slots in a screen, but it cannot explain why the photon goes through the particular slot it goes through. The arguments in favour of humans having thisness have the consequence that which soul comes into existence as the result of the development of some foetus is another phenomenon which is not explicable by laws of nature. Because humans have thisness, there could not be a full scientific explanation of the existence of any particular soul and so of any particular human being. Science can tell us that, when a human foetus has reached a certain stage of development, it will cause the existence of a soul, but it cannot tell us which soul that will be. It is not because of the backwardness of contemporary science, but because of the very nature of a scientific explanation—that it explains by laws which connect substances in virtue of their properties—that there cannot be a full scientific explanation of why I or any of my readers exist at all.

Notes

1. Introduction

1. I have argued for my view on this topic over many years in articles in philosophical journals, in half of a book (co-authored with Sydney Shoemaker) *Personal Identity* (1984), and in two full-length books (*The Evolution of the Soul* (1986) and *Mind, Brain, and Free Will* (2013)). As well as being intended as an exposition for a wider public of the central theses of that view, the present book includes some important developments of earlier versions. Some of *Mind, Brain, and Free Will* was concerned with whether humans have (as I believe) free will. In order to make the present book fairly short, I shall not discuss that issue in this book. I am very grateful to Mark Wynn and to three anonymous referees for detailed comments on previous drafts of this book, and to Peter Momtchiloff for ushering yet another book of mine through the OUP publication process. Material that originally appeared in *Mind, Brain, and Free Will* by Richard Swinburne (2013) is reproduced by permission of Oxford University Press: https://global.oup.com/academic/product/mind-brain-and-free-will-9780199662579. Thanks to Wiley-Blackwell for permission to use in Chapter 4 some of the material of a paper: 'Cartesian Substance Dualism' by Richard Swinburne, published in (eds.) Jonathan J. Loose, Angus J. L. Menuge, and J.P. Moreland, *The Blackwell Companion to Substance Dualism* (2018), Wiley-Blackwell, doi:10.1002/9781119468004.ch9.
2. John Searle, *Mind: A Brief Introduction*, Oxford University Press, 2004, p. 48.

2. Physicalism and Property Dualism

1. Philosophers call this kind of consciousness 'phenomenal consciousness', and distinguish it from what they call 'access consciousness'. Someone has 'access consciousness' to some item of information if they take account of that item in achieving some purpose; they may not be at all aware (and so phenomenally conscious) of using that item of information.
2. Thomas Nagel, 'What is it like to be a bat?', republished in his *Mortal Questions*, Cambridge University Press, 1979, p. 166.
3. So to say that a sentence and the proposition which it expresses is 'conceivable' is not just to say that people can suppose it to be true, but

to say that they can suppose it to be true without thereby implying a contradiction. If someone supposes some sentence to be conceivable when really it is not conceivable, that sentence is only 'apparently conceivable'.

4. The proposition that some property A is the same property as some property B is normally expressed by a sentence of the form 'A is B'. But not all such sentences express an identity between the property of being A and the property of being B. In some such sentences 'A' is being used to pick out a property which itself has the property of being A, and/or 'B' is being used to pick out a property which itself has the property of being B. Thus 'the colour of the walls is Amanda's favourite colour' does not say that the property of being the colour of the walls is the same property as the property of being Amanda's favourite colour, but rather that that colour property which has the property of being Amanda's favourite colour property is the same colour property as the colour property which the walls have—which might be, for example, the property of being green. The definition of property identity—that two properties are the same iff having one property makes the same difference to a substance as does having the other property—is concerned with an identity between properties, whether or not the properties are picked out by what is essential to them or by some non-essential property of that property (for example, whether the property green is picked out by 'green' or by 'Amanda's favourite colour'). In terms of a distinction which I shall introduce in Chapter 5, a property picked out by a predicate 'A' is the same as a property picked out by a predicate 'B' iff when 'A' is replaced by a co-referring informative designator 'C', and 'B' is replaced by a co-referring informative designator 'D', 'C is D' is logically necessary.

5. That is, their occurrence makes the same difference in the actual world where 'London' and 'The 2018 capital of the UK' refer to the same city. The referents of the expressions in the descriptions of the event, which refer to substances, are the substances to which they refer in the actual world. There are other 'possible worlds' (= logically possible states of affairs) where London is not the capital of the UK in 2018, and then 'London' and 'The 2018 capital of the UK' would not refer to the same substance.

6. Most definitions of 'supervene' (and cognate words) in philosophy books and articles define 'property A supervenes on property B' in terms of metaphysical necessity, along such lines as 'it is metaphysically necessary that any substance which has B has A because it has B, but not metaphysically necessary that any substance which has A has B', and provide a similar kind of definition for the supervenience of one event on another event. Metaphysical necessity is supposed to be the strongest kind of necessity there can be; it includes logical necessity, but it also includes metaphysical

necessity of a different kind. I have tried to produce a definition of 'supervene' which avoids the use of the technical term 'metaphysically necessary', but which—I believe—brings out what is involved in the above technical definition. In providing a definition of 'metaphysically necessary' in terms of 'logically necessary', I am assuming that any metaphysically possible world is also a logically possible world (and conversely). (As David Chalmers wrote, 'the relevant space of worlds is the same in both cases'—see his *The Conscious Mind*, Oxford University Press, 1996, p. 68.) I provide my account of the metaphysical necessity of propositions in the Appendix to Chapter 5, using the concept of an 'informative designator' which I define in that chapter.

7. In this book I am treating physicalism merely as a doctrine about the nature of human beings, even though most of those who are physicalists about human beings hold that everything else in the universe is also physical, and so—for example—hold that there is no God.

8. David Lewis, *On the Plurality of Worlds*, Basil Blackwell, 1986, p. 14.

9. In writing this I am assuming that electrons do not have 'thisness'; I explain what I mean by this term and why I am making this assumption in Chapter 7.

10. I write 'normally' because there are some 'neutral properties' which are such that whether a substance having such a property is a physical event or a mental event depends on the nature of the substance. Thus the disjunctive property of 'either being 6 foot high or thinking about philosophy' is a neutral property. This is because me having that property is a mental event, since I can know better than can anyone else whether I have that property (since I can know better than can anyone else whether I have one of the two disjuncts that constitute the whole disjunctive property—I can know better whether I'm thinking about philosophy); but the gatepost having that property is a physical event (since no one can know better than can anyone else whether or not it has either of the two disjuncts).

11. Most philosophers call what I am calling 'propositional events' 'intentional events'. But that is misleading because it confuses the whole class of such events with 'intentions' which are only one kind of such events.

12. Since bodies have physical properties, having a body as at least a part of oneself entails having physical properties; and to have physical properties entails having at least a public part, one equally accessible to all— which is what one's body is.

3. Theories of Personal Identity

1. See for example Charles Choi, 'Strange but true: when half a brain is better than a whole one', *Scientific American*, May 24, 2007.

2. John Locke, *Essay Concerning Human Understanding*, 2.27.19.
3. Thomas Reid, *Essays on the Powers of the Human Mind*, III, ch. 6.
4. David Lewis, 'Survival and identity', *Philosophical Papers*, vol. I, Oxford University Press, 1983.
5. Robert Nozick, 'The identity of the self' in his *Philosophical Explanations*, Oxford University Press, 1981.
6. Harold Noonan, *Personal Identity*, Routledge, 1989, ch. 6.
7. Derek Parfit, *Reasons and Persons*, Oxford University Press, 1984, Part III.
8. Parfit, *Reasons and Persons*, p. 239.

4. Descartes's Argument for the Soul

1. I get this example and the principle it supports from André Gallois, *Occasions of Identity*, Oxford University Press, 1998, p. 251. I am grateful to Eric Olson for this way of expressing the principle, instead of a more complicated way which I used previously.
2. *The Philosophical Works of Descartes*, translated by E.S. Haldane and G.R.T. Ross, Cambridge University Press, vol. 1, 1968, p. 101.
3. Paul Snowdon, *Persons, Animals, Ourselves*, Oxford University Press, 2014, p. 48.
4. *Principles of Philosophy*, Principle 9. Translation from *The Philosophical Works of Descartes*, vol. 1, p. 222.
5. See his *Reply to Objections* V. Translation from *The Philosophical Works of Descartes*, vol. 2, pp. 210–11.
6. See Aquinas, *Summa Theologiae* Ia.75.4 ad 2.
7. See Aquinas, *Commentary on I Corinthians* 15, lectio 2, *anima mea non est ego*, 'my soul is not me'.
8. See Aquinas, *Summa Contra Gentiles*, 4.92.

5. We Know Who We Are

1. In previous writings of mine I expounded the distinction between 'informative designators' and 'uninformative designators' as a distinction between two kinds of what philosophers call 'rigid designators'. In the main argument of this book I have expounded the distinction between 'informative designators' and 'uninformative designators' in a wider way which does not use the concept of a 'rigid designator'. For those interested, I explain this concept in the Appendix to this chapter and show how it enables us to understand concepts of 'metaphysical' modality.
2. David Chalmers, *The Character of Consciousness*, Oxford University Press, 2010, p. 49.

3. I wrote '*little* room for serious doubt' because there is always the theoretical possibility that others may be using the words denoting kinds of propositional events, such as 'desire' and 'intention', in different senses from each other which cannot be publicly detected. But I suggest that it is most unlikely that any initial differences in the ways in which people understand such words cannot be corrected by pointing out the logical connections between such words and public behaviour (for example, that beliefs together with intentions entail public behaviour in those who have the requisite physical capacity, in the way analysed in Chapter 2). Sensations, unlike propositional events, have only contingent connections with public events.

4. Sydney Shoemaker, 'Introspection and the Self' in (ed.) Q. Cassam, *Self-Knowledge*, Oxford University Press, 1994, p. 82.

5. David Hume, *A Treatise of Human Nature*, Book 1, part 4, section 6.

6. Max Black, 'The identity of indiscernibles', *Mind* 61 (1952) 153–64; see p. 156.

7. Since a 'property', as I expounded this concept, is a universal, that is such as could be possessed by a different substance other than any substance which has it, such expressions as 'being identical to Anastasia' do not denote a property, because no one else could have had that property except Anastasia. Also, I am assuming in my account of the identity of indiscernibles and so of 'thisness' that the 'relational properties' of a substance are understood as properties relating that substance to other substances, individuated only by their properties, for example the property of being two miles away from a sphere with such-and-such properties. Otherwise, if we assume, following Black, that there could be two spheres of the kind which he described, then we could individuate them by their names—say, 'Castor' and 'Pollux', and then each would have a property not possessed by the other. Castor would have the property of being two miles away from Pollux, but Pollux would not have this property.

8. The 'Principle of the Identity of Indiscernibles' which I claim to be false must be distinguished from the 'Principle of the Identity of Composites' which I discussed in Chapter 4, and claim to be true. The 'Principle of the Identity of Indiscernibles' is concerned both with what makes non-composite substances (= substances which do not have parts) the substances they are, and with what makes the parts of composite substances separate parts (that is, themselves separate substances). The principle of the identity of composites applies only to substances which have more than one part, each of which is itself a substance; it claims that if the parts are the same (and it provides no criteria for their being the same), and have the same properties (essential and non-essential) at all times, then the composite substance is the same.

6. Souls and Bodies Interact

1. In the sense that they are probable overall, given the degree of probability of the basic belief and the degree to which the basic belief makes that non-basic belief probable. So if we have some basic belief which we believe to be only slightly more probable than not, and we believe that that basic belief makes some other proposition only slightly more probable than not, we will not believe that that other proposition is overall probable, and so we will not hold it as a non-basic belief.

2. There are many different senses of 'rational' or 'justified' in which a belief can be rational or justified. I am concerned only with a belief being justified in the sense of being a rational response at the time of the belief to the evidence available to the believer. For the many different senses of 'rational' or 'justified', see my *Epistemic Justification*, Oxford University Press, 2001, chapters 6 and 7.

3. In my *Mind, Brain, and Free Will* (Oxford University Press, 2013, p. 56) I advocated a 'principle of testimony' that it is always rational to believe what someone else tells you—in the absence of counter-evidence. Although I still hold that principle, all I am claiming here is that if it seems that someone is telling me something, it is rational to believe that she is telling me something. I do not depend on the principle that it is always rational to believe that what she is telling me is true.

4. For example, a patient from whom portions of both temporal lobes including their hippocampus were removed proved unable to recall anything which had happened to him more than a few minutes earlier. For a description of this patient's condition see, among many other places, R.F. Thompson, *The Brain*, Worth Publishers, 3rd edition, 2000, pp. 392–3.

5. This is basically the position of Jaegwon Kim. See his *Physicalism or Something Near Enough*, Princeton University Press, 2005.

6. For Libet's own account of his work, see B. Libet, *Mind Time*, Harvard University Press, 2004, ch. 4. For a more recent account of this work see W.P. Banks and S. Pockett, 'Benjamin Libet's work on the neuroscience of free will' in (eds.) M. Velmans and S. Schneider, *The Blackwell Companion to Consciousness*, Wiley-Blackwell, 2009. Libet's work and its developments are often cited as showing that humans do not have free will. The justification provided for this claim is that this work has shown that all our actions are caused by brain events without any intervention by conscious events. I claim to have shown that this supposed justification is false, but I do not discuss in this book whether it can be shown that we do or do not have free will on the basis of other arguments.

7. H.L. Roediger, M.K. Goode, and F.M. Zaromb, 'Free will and the control of action' in (eds.) J. Baer, J.C. Kaufman, and R.F. Baumeister, *Are We Free?*, Oxford University Press, 2008. For similar quotations from other neuroscientists see A.R. Mele, *Effective Intentions*, Oxford University Press, 2009, pp. 70–3.

8. I consider (in *Mind, Brain, and Free Will*, pp. 117–23) a suggestion that it may be possible to learn about such events without presupposing mental-to-physical causation by modifying our understanding of 'memory' and 'testimony', in such a way that we could be said to 'remember' some past physical event without assuming that this involves remembering a past experience of it; and in such a way that we could be said to give 'testimony' to the occurrence of a past event without assuming that that involves testifying to a past experience of that event. But calculations are mental events; and so apparent memory of them and belief in apparent testimony about them presuppose mental-to-physical causation.

9. For a summary of proposals in the scientific literature for how Quantum theory can allow for some mental-to-physical causation, see my *Mind, Brain, and Free Will*, pp. 112–17.

7. Could Science Explain Souls?

1. I have considered elsewhere what constitutes good evidence for the truth of a revelation purportedly from God, including revelation about life after death. See, for example, my book *Was Jesus God?*, Oxford University Press, 2008.

2. See, for example, the article by Christof Koch, 'When does consciousness arise in human babies?', *Scientific American*, September 2009.

3. For argument that a simpler theory is, as such, more probably the true theory than is a more complicated theory, see my *Epistemic Justification*, Oxford University Press, 2001, pp. 83–102.

4. For more details of multiple personality cases, and reasons for interpreting them as changes in the beliefs and desires of a single person (and so, in my view, of a single soul), see Tim Bayne, *The Unity of Consciousness*, Oxford University Press, 2010, pp. 162–71.

5. R.W. Sperry, 'Hemisphere DeConnection and unity in conscious awareness', *American Psychologist* 23 (1968) 723–33.

6. For full details of the 'split-brain' phenomenon and comparison of the evidence favouring different interpretations of it, see Bayne, *The Unity of Consciousness*, chapter 9.

7. See Roland Puccetti, 'Brain bisection and personal identity', *British Journal for the Philosophy of Science* 24 (1973) 339–55.

8. For details of the state of PVS patients, assessment of the worth of the evidence from their brain events in response to questions, and the worth of the different legal criteria for death, see the papers in (ed.) W. Sinnnot-Armstrong, *Finding Consciousness*, Oxford University Press, 2016.

9. A few contemporary Christian philosophers have claimed that physicalism is compatible with humans continuing to live after death when the physical matter of which their bodies were composed becomes a corpse and decomposes or is reduced to ashes by being burnt in the crematorium. For, those philosophers claim, maybe at death our physical bodies are duplicated, being split into two bodies, so that while the matter of one body becomes a corpse, another body is created at the same time, and this second body continues to exist in some faraway place, or in a place in another dimension of space. In that way every human would continue to exist as a physical substance. See, for example, Dean Zimmerman, 'The compatibility of materialism and survival: the "falling elevator model"', *Faith and Philosophy* 16 (1999) 194–212. I consider this a wild physical theory which could only be justified if there was both strong evidence against substance dualism and for life after death. But, as I have argued in this book, since there is very strong evidence for substance dualism, I suggest that we should reject this 'wild' theory.

10. For an account of the very limited results to date of the work of neuroscientists in this field, and the obstacles to further progress, see the papers by John Dylan-Haynes ('Brain reading') and Tim Bayne ('How to read minds') in (eds.) S. Richmond and others, *I Know What You Are Thinking*, Oxford University Press, 2012.

11. For a quick survey of such theories see the article in the (online) *Stanford Encyclopaedia of Philosophy* on 'Consciousness' (revised 2014) by Robert van Gulick, sections 9.5 to 9.8.

12. In his well-known paper 'What is it like to be a bat?' (republished in his *Mortal Questions*, Cambridge University Press, 1979) Thomas Nagel drew our attention to the fact that the auditory experiences of bats perceiving the presence of objects must be very different from the visual experiences other mammals have when they perceive objects.

13. Two of the theories about the brain basis of consciousness referred to in note 11 currently taken seriously are the 'global workplace theory' and the 'information integration theory'. While the global workplace theory seems to have application only to systems of neurons connected in the kind of way that the neurons of our brains are connected, the

information integration theory claims that consciousness arises in any system in which 'information' is integrated in a particular kind of way, and so seems to allow that consciousness could arise in any system in which the parts are connected in a certain kind of way.

14. See Thomas Aquinas, *Summa Theologiae*, Ia.118.2 ad 2.

Guide to Further Reading

The view of the nature of human beings advocated in this book is, as I have emphasized throughout, very different from the views of most contemporary scientists and philosophers. So the reader will need to compare it with rival views. Two introductions to the spectrum of views on this topic, reaching different conclusions, are:

Barry Dainton, *Self*, Penguin Books, 2014 (wide-ranging, intended for non-philosophers, easy to read).

Ian Ravenscroft, *Philosophy of Mind: A Beginner's Guide*, Oxford University Press, 2005 (very clear and concise).

For a defence of physicalism (expounded in my Chapter 2), see:

David Papineau, *Thinking about Consciousness*, Oxford University Press, 2002.

For an anthology containing influential recent book chapters and articles advocating 'complex' theories of personal identity (expounded in my Chapter 3), together with a long introduction describing the history of theories of personal identity up to the end of the twentieth century, see:

J. Martin and J. Barresi (eds.), *Personal Identity*, Blackwell Publishing, 2003.

For a recent anthology of articles defending and opposing substance dualism, see:

J.J. Loose and others (eds.), *The Blackwell Companion to Substance Dualism*, Wiley-Blackwell, 2018.

For details of the neuroscience underlying the research programme developed from the work of Benjamin Libet (described in my Chapter 6), which many have interpreted as showing that our conscious intentions do not influence our brain events, see:

Sean A. Spence, *The Actor's Brain*, Oxford University Press, 2009.

And for philosophical commentary on this programme, see:

Alfred R. Mele, *Effective Intentions*, Oxford University Press, 2009.

Two books, very important for this topic, although philosophically some-what more difficult than the others, are:

Saul Kripke, *Naming and Necessity*, Blackwell Publishing, 1981. (This introduces the concept of a 'rigid designator', defends the view that there are necessary propositions which are not 'logically' necessary, and uses these results to defend the view that mental events are not identical to brain events.)

David Chalmers, *The Conscious Mind*, Oxford University Press, 1996. (A classical defence of mere property dualism.)

Index